"An Improbable School" gives us all a gli...
students collaborate to take charge of
and Paul tell the story of an exemplary school, challenging
demonstrating innovative practices and why they matter. In a time of turmoil and change,
"An Improbable School" offers inspiration and direction to those who care deeply about
the future of education.

Dr. Heather Terrill Stotts, Executive Director, Innovative Schools Network

An Improbable School

by
Paul Tweed &
Liz Seubert

LeadPath

An Improbable School ...

I came across a quote by John Taylor Gatto, who is a retired school teacher and an activist against traditional schooling, that said "we could encourage the best qualities of youthfulness—curiosity, adventure, resilience, the capacity for surprising insight—simply by being more flexible about time, texts, and tests, by introducing kids to truly competent adults, and by giving each student the autonomy he or she needs in order to take a risk every now and then. But we don't do that (*Weapons of Mass Instruction*, 2009)."

John Taylor Gatto had clearly never heard of Wildlands, the school where we do that.

I came to Wildlands as a junior after spending the previous sixteen years at a traditional public school. The biggest surprise that came with the switch was being able to say that I love school. Over the course of my two years here, **I've developed a passion for learning that I never would have thought possible two years ago**. When given the opportunity to learn about things that interest you, learning becomes exciting. When you design your own projects, you gain creativity and the ability to think outside the box. When you get to decide the most efficient way to manage your time, you become independent and self-disciplined. When you design or participate in group projects, you gain leadership and teamwork skills. When you are presented with a world of opportunity instead of a strict curriculum, your mind is expanded instead of controlled.

So as a senior about to go on to college, I can say that as well as preparing me academically, my experience at Wildlands has prepared me mentally by exposing me to these skills that are necessary for success in college, careers, and life in general.

When I look back on my time at Wildlands, I could pretty easily sum it up in two words: new experiences. Wildlands is filled to the brim with new and unique experiences. Whether they're fun, challenging, scary, or all of the above, every type of experience is valuable—even the "bad" ones end in an important lesson ...

... Most of the fear that typically comes with graduation is fear of not being prepared for what comes next. I think I can speak for everyone graduating with me tonight when I say that we are very lucky to not have that fear. Although some of us may not know what comes next, uncertainty isn't something to fear when we know we possess the skills, experience, and knowledge that will help us excel at whatever it may be.

Molly Dexter, Class of 2013,
Graduation Speech at Wildlands School,
May 23, 2013

Contents

Introduction

What Do You Teach?

When I meet people for the first time, I can't wait until someone asks, "So, Liz, what do you do?" Honestly, this is usually my favorite part of the conversation, since with a bit of a grin and a whole lot of pride, I say, "I'm a teacher and I love what I do."

The best part, though, comes with the inevitable follow-up question, "What do you teach?" Often I'll ask, "How much time do you have?" and really set people up, because when I explain that I teach at a teacher-powered, science-research, project-based school with sixty students on a 400-acre nature reserve, the looks on their faces tell me they didn't get the "I teach third grade" response they'd expected. Well, they *asked*! And, by the time they listen to just a snippet of the projects I work on with my students, people either wonder why they didn't get to go to a school like Wildlands or wish they could sign up to take classes! Just hearing about the impressive projects our Wildlands students undertake seems to re-ignite everybody's love of learning—and a whole lot of curiosity.

That, in a nutshell, is the reason for this book.

We Teach Children

After almost ten years of increased inquiries about Wildlands—how it operates, what our students do, how we manage it all—we (Paul Tweed and Liz Seubert, Wildlands teachers) decided that we couldn't just hide in the woods anymore. This book exists because we want to share our journey to build not only a school, but a school culture and learning environment unmatched in our area. Through this book we'll do our best to explain how "Wildlands: The Idea" became "Wildlands: The Reality."

This book is not meant to provide a magic formula to reform all schools or a solution for all educational ills. We know not all schools need to be the same. But we also know that students deserve learning environments that fit their needs, learning styles, and personalities. More than anything, we know that our goal is to teach *children*, not curriculum. We believe that choice is important, options are critical, and that students and their families deserve both.

Wildlands is a public, locally governed, teacher-managed charter school within the Augusta, Wisconsin, School District, and part of a growing group of schools that provides students and families with different educational offerings. We are not part of any charter management organization, and any student may apply to attend *free of charge* through a lottery process. Simply put, Wildlands is an option, a public school opportunity that students can choose to try, stick with, or move on from.

You won't find traditional teacher-led classes, assigned seats, or bubble tests at Wildlands. School supplies include items like bug spray, sunscreen, extra clothes in preparation for inclement weather, and warm boots in the winter. There are no bells to tell our students when to move from one room or activity to the next. Students don't receive ID numbers, locker numbers, or library cards. Instead they check out things like computers, camping supplies, GPS units, and video cameras through a spreadsheet and our honor system. When visitors walk through our doors, they are greeted by our students, not a secretary.

Wildlands was created because, as experienced educators, we discovered that students excel when they are part of the plan, part of the project, and part of the team instead of passive receivers of a curriculum. With this as our guide—in addition to working to connect students to real community issues—we use projects and project-based learning as a focal point for the school. Our central focus at Wildlands is to treat each student as an *individual*—a valued member of our family—and not only as a member of a class or part of a list of standards that need to be checked off.

We have much more respect for our students than to reduce them to test scores at some state or national level. That said, our students are tested *daily* as they need to be fully vested in their own educational program. They present to peers and the public, revise, edit, improve upon, and produce projects that are connected to the community and have meaningful results outside of school. They develop, practice, and demonstrate leadership and personal management skills that are central to being independent lifelong learners. Wildlands students live in a formative assessment world, consistently striving for learning and outcomes at their personal best.

We know that we have to prove ourselves as a school to educational traditionalists and others who have stayed "inside the box." That's okay with us. We welcome evaluation, scrutiny, and want transparency and accountability. To be afforded flexibility in our school, we believe that we need to show a higher level of student success than the traditional school environment, so a wide variety of assessments are included in our school model. Since we opened the school, **our students have participated in all assessments required by the state and local school district and have consistently performed far above state averages.** We also know that a single test does not make or break an education, nor does it measure real success or personal growth. Our students and families realize this, too, and Wildlands concentrates on much more than content and testing. We treat assessment—and everything—very differently.

Since starting Wildlands ten years ago, we have been thinking, questioning, and restructuring our school every single day in order to reach out to students in a different way. In this book, you will read about the evolution of Wildlands and the lessons we have learned along the way. (We are learners, too, and we don't profess to know it all.) Our experiences illustrate that performance, projects, community involvement, authentic research, and personally relevant learning can be done. Additionally, we want to share our individual and joint perspectives on how Wildlands was shaped, and our greatest hope is that our story inspires your own love for learning—and teaching.

After reading this book we hope you will understand that schools don't all have to be the same. There are many important factors that come into play when designing and operating schools that work to meet student needs. We will introduce what we have found to be the essentials for transforming our school into a student-centered learning culture. Above all, we hope you come to realize there are many ways to view learning, and all children deserve opportunities to develop real relationships with their schools, value what they do, be challenged, develop confidence, have adventures in learning, and be rooted in a supportive and safe place.

Part I

We Can Do *What?*

chapter 1

Change the
Questions

Educational reform has most often come from the top down. Most recently, the Common Core Standards movement has been in the spotlight, but by the time you read this book it will have faded, disappeared, or have been replaced by the next *new* thing in education. Rewind the clock and take a ride on the merry-go-round of educational reform, and you'll find that there have been more than a few "cutting-edge" movements: State Standards, No Child Left Behind, Educator Effectiveness, A Nation at Risk, etc. All are top-down, umbrella-level "solutions" to our collective educational woes. Unfortunately, they also tend to be shortsighted, dealing with the content—the knowledge and skills of learning—but fail to even mention the *culture* of learning. This "reform" simply shifts the overall target to a few new (or reworded) goals, but *doesn't seek to change the way schools operate*. In fact, during the past thirty years, educators have seen at least five or more of these reform movements come and go with very little change in most schools—except that more students seem to disengage from learning *at a younger age*.

This is a travesty!

Perhaps the whole idea of "reform" needs to be reformed. Perhaps policy makers and some educators are simply asking the wrong questions. **Maybe we should begin by asking what we want from education in the first place.** Isn't it a citizenry prepared to learn? Confident, independent, hard-working people? People with *can-do* attitudes who've learned that service to one's community is a cornerstone of our free democratic society? People who can solve problems and be creative or innovative? People who can overcome failure? We could go on and on.

So what's the point here? The point is that the educational system in our country has been focusing on content knowledge, tests, scores, curriculum-delivery systems, published materials and texts, prescriptive remediation—and measuring success with a single, narrow yardstick. By doing this, we've actually turned away many students and given them good reasons to dislike learning. Many students feel they are failures because they don't do well on tests. Others who are talented in areas outside the testing spectrum often have no way to demonstrate their strengths. By focusing on content instead of people, society has created a system that provides few options for diversity and treats all students as if they are the same in ability, social status, interest, passion, and aptitude.

It is time to change the questions we ask about education.

We need to stop asking how we can improve or reform our current practices and start asking how we can create NEW systems and practices for twenty-first-century students, families, communities, and economies. Back when cars were first hitting the assembly line, Henry Ford no longer needed people with saddle-making skills. The same is true now for education. Big shifts in society, environment, and the economy call for equally big shifts in how we prepare our children. Education and legislators have to realize the nineteenth-century model served its purpose, but it is time to move on and re-examine learning *from the student's perspective.*

Uncommon

Creating a school where the students are the center and their needs, interests, and abilities drive the planning—and learning—is a significant challenge that develops independent, responsible learners. Over the years, we have seen our Wildlands students become a learning community—a family—and valuable functioning members of our school and local community. During this journey, we have identified several qualities that are essential for creating a school culture that is welcoming, owned by the students, and fosters community-based, independent learners. If this is the type of learning environment you want to create, the best advice we can give is the focus of this book: seven essentials for transforming how teachers teach and students learn.

Relationships
Values
Opportunity
Adventure
Challenge
Confidence
Place

All are powerful words in their own right. All are powerful standards if a school uses them to create a learning culture centered on *students'* needs. These seven essentials for transforming school culture are about students, not about content. They are about learning, living, growing, becoming a part of a community, developing into independent learners, and having fun along the way. They are rooted in mutual respect between student and teacher and provide an environment that is psychologically and physically safe. These essentials are big-picture ideas that schools can focus on to build places where students can risk making a mistake or being wrong without fear of being judged or ridiculed. We don't mean to say that these words should be listed on a poster board in the corner of the room for everyone to see. They need to be lived, breathed, and believed by everyone in the room at all times, or it won't work.

Challenge the Status Quo

Change only happens when we challenge the status quo and deliver successful student results. At Wildlands we have found, firsthand, some small kernels of truth in the successful results category. Wildlands has demonstrated that high expectations in an inquiry-based model of learning build the required twenty-first-century skills, but even more importantly, develop the social skills and personal confidence that are required for continued lifelong learning. If educators are going to change lives, students need to be treated as living, breathing, feeling, and growing people. Students can learn, thrive, laugh, enjoy school, and be contributing members of a community and school, as they should be.

To do so, first the overall focus must be the student, the entire student, and each student as an individual. Only then can we get to that stuff called content, skills, and process. You want change in learning? Involve the students, do something real, and train teachers to work with students instead of controlling them. Get rid of the stale rows of desks—or even the classroom—and dump the century-old factory model of schooling.

Information is everywhere and multiplying exponentially every year. Real learning can't be accomplished in an assembly line model anymore. Society says it wants high functioning young adults. Employers want employees who can solve problems, think critically, collaborate with others, be innovative and creative, and have adaptable skill sets that involve lifelong learning. How do we get that? Can educators really achieve twenty-first-century results with methods developed in the nineteenth-century disguised as a new list of what students should know and do? This makes as much sense as trying to fix a cell phone with the tools and methods found in Edison's lab!

The most difficult part in breaking the old (current) mold is to get others in the world of education to say, "Hey, we want that new way!" for their students and schools. New and effective ways of working with students ARE out there, and have successful results to back them up, but getting an entire district, or even a school, to get on board doesn't seem to happen often. Sadly, it's much easier to just follow directions, but people don't come with directions. The only common thing we all really have when it comes to learning, interests, personality, attitudes, and aptitudes, is that we are all uncommon.

When presented with the opportunity to develop a new school with new ideals, a different way of teaching and challenging students revealed itself and quickly became essential practice at Wildlands.

It Isn't Rocket Science

When I was a graduate student at the University of Iowa, my office was in a building named after a very successful physics professor, James Van Allen. The name may sound vaguely familiar because the radiation belts that surround Earth were named after him, as he was the one who discovered them. To me, he was the stereotypical "rocket scientist," but also as down-to-earth and cordial as they come. It just so happened that Professor Van Allen had an office down the hall from mine. We used to bump into each other in the lunchroom or hallway, chat about the Hawkeye football team, and over time I got to know him well enough to call him Jim.

One day, he and I were talking about education. I told him some of my instructors had mentioned they'd asked him what he looks for in a good physics student. As a world-class physicist, he wanted world-class students, right? Because I have always been a bit of a skeptic and sometimes thought my course lecturers spun a few yarns to make a point, I decided to ask Professor Van Allen directly what he looks for in a student. (I guess that is my science background, looking for independent confirmation.)

His answer surprised me a little. I was fully expecting him to answer that he would like the students to be well prepared in the sciences, have a substantial physics background, be strong in math, include high ACT and SAT scores, and possess impeccable research skills. Instead, I got something entirely different. Van Allen (and I paraphrase from memory here) answered, "I look for people who are interested in learning, curious, happy, and upbeat to work with. I like to work with students who love learning. I can take people and teach them all sorts of physics and math, but they first have to be someone who will work hard, think creatively, and have a good sense of humor. Good people are hard to find."

Huh?

He didn't say he wanted expert high school physics students. He didn't reference science bowl competition winners, or anyone of the sort. Nothing was mentioned about ACT scores or grade point averages. Most of what Van Allen talked about circled around the topics of good citizenry, good attitude, work ethic, and happy, well-adjusted, curious people who like to learn. People ready to pursue their goals and dreams. He wanted students who were independent and could learn, instead of being just taught.

I know Van Allen was onto something: focus on developing high quality people who enjoy what they do, have interests and curiosity about learning, and let them find their path in life. Let students explore and find it for themselves—exactly the opposite of telling them what to do or to make them listen and repeat. Basic skills, competencies, and knowledge are all critically important, but by emphasizing only those, we shortchange our students. **It is essential that we find ways for students to learn to love learning.**

chapter 2

Something Different

The Path to Wildlands

The journey to Wildlands started with a simple question posed by the district administrator while I was teaching science at Augusta High School. "Paul, if you could do one thing to take your science program to the next level, what would it be?" he asked. "I would like a bus," I answered without skipping a beat, explaining our program's fieldwork and how a mobile lab would get students into the field more often. Not too long after that conversation, I received a phone call. It was the district administrator: I got a bus. My jaw dropped. This news began a new path in education I would never had dreamed possible.

The bus I was given had been taken out of daily route service by the transportation department. It was still safe, made it from Point A to Point B, and would serve as a GIANT project for kids to turn into a rolling science lab and classroom on wheels. Five months later, after receiving a massive overhaul by a team of students assisted by the educational technology teacher with funds that were awarded from two grants I had written, the Augusta Science Mobile Lab was born—and so was the freedom to involve students in field research and take learning beyond the classroom walls.

As the program evolved, we partnered with the Wisconsin Department of Natural Resources (WDNR), Eau Claire County Conservation Department, the Lake Eau Claire Association, and other outdoor sports and conservation organizations to conduct field research on relevant local issues during summer school and the normal school year. Students worked on meaningful science issues with a variety of partners in the professional and volunteer world. Projects were designed with community connections and professional mentors as a cornerstone, and many students came back year after year to work on lakes, streams, forests, and wildlife projects.

Wildlands: The Idea

The success of our program led to another question, this time from a school board member who asked, "Paul, could you see developing a charter school that works with students for the full school day and not just a couple hours or only during the summer school program?"

His question was prompted by the Wisconsin Department of Public Instruction's effort into what some had called "entrepreneurial education." The DPI was using federal funding to help districts develop new schools utilizing innovative methods to meet students' needs. Many charter schools around the state had impressive designs to serve students in all areas, from the arts to technology, science, and everything in between. The first thing that came to my mind was, "Wow, that school day would have to be drastically different." The next thing was, "Where do we start?"

A great deal of learning happened over the next year as we planned the opening of Wildlands. Here are the most important things we learned:

1. School design is paramount. We learned by visiting those who had forged the trail before us and adapted what we learned to meet our vision. Every school we visited was crafted to meet the needs of its particular community.

2. Define what you want for your students. When visiting schools, we were greeted and hosted by students who were dynamic, interested, engaged, and communicated clearly. We wanted that for our students. It was apparent the students we met really *liked* being at their schools.

3. Relationships are key. Without forming many partnerships, our school would not be what it is. Working with the Augusta School District, Beaver Creek Reserve, neighboring schools, state and local resource agencies, community groups, and individuals has cast a wide web of support for the school.

4. Start-up funding is necessary. Because Wildlands started from ideas, visions, and dreams, it was absolutely necessary to have outside funding to create it. The Wisconsin Department of Public Instruction's Charter School Grant Program made it possible for this school to exist and develop into what it is today.

5. Project-based learning provides a context to build a school with high expectations for independence and responsibility on the part of the students. We will talk much more about project-based learning at Wildlands, but suffice it to say, without it, our school could not be what it is today.

Wildlands: The Reality

In the fall of 2005, the Wildlands Science Research Charter School opened, welcoming forty students from grades 7 and 8 and grades 11 and 12. Those first students arrived with curiosity about what they had signed up for, and soon a diverse, small school learning community formed and has continued ever since. Wildlands has enrolled students from Augusta, Fall Creek, Eau Claire, Menomonie, Altoona, Chippewa

Falls, Osseo-Fairchild, New Auburn, and Eleva. Today, we have sixty students in grades 7 through 12, and the majority of our group activities focus on the investigation of the natural world. Wildlands has a unique partnership with Beaver Creek Reserve (BCR), a 400-acre nature center in the Eau Claire County Forest. The school is located on that property and works regularly with the BCR staff on projects.

Much of what takes place in the core subjects of math, science, social studies, English, physical education, and recreation also centers around a project theme. Students read, write, investigate, report, speak, investigate the history of, and present results of projects related to a theme. Students gradually move toward more independence as they learn and adapt to the project environment. Examples of high-school learning projects connected to community issues are as follows:

Bathymetric Mapping of Fall Creek Pond. This project integrated geography skills, GPS technology, Geographic Information Systems (GIS) computer technology, geometry, math, and statistical skills to develop a new depth map of a local pond to replace the 1960 DNR map.

Mark and Recapture Population Studies. Various species such as raccoon, squirrel, fish, and others have been live trapped, tagged, and population models applied to collected data.

Radio Telemetry Range and Habitat Studies. Species including bears, raccoons, coyotes, deer, roughed grouse, and northern pike have been radio tagged. Students have worked in the areas of live trapping, safe handling of animals, radio collaring, signal location and processing, and GIS computer models to plot range and habitat use.

Lake Eau Claire Bathymetric Mapping Project. A comprehensive bathymetric map was developed with GPS, GIS, and handheld computer technology. This project was funded by the Wisconsin DNR and conducted in cooperation with the Lake Eau Claire Association and the U.S. Army Corps of Engineers. The results of this study were used to help guide the management of the lake water-quality issues.

Stream Habitat and Water Quality Studies. Students worked with ongoing studies of local creeks and streams and have performed habitat analysis, water chemistry, fish population, and invertebrate studies.

Inventory and Identification of Algae Species in Lake Eau Claire. Student work centered around sampling the lake for as many algae species as could be found. Both identification and calculation of the relative amounts of algae were done.

Small Mammal Inventory Project. In cooperation with the Aquatic and Terrestrial Resources Inventory section of the Wisconsin DNR, students developed small mammal hair traps, taxonomic keys to mammal hair at the microscopic level, and a DNA analysis library of small mammal species differences for identification purposes.

Construction Projects. Students have designed and built facilities for the charter school and Beaver Creek Reserve as part of construction technology and service learning.

Forestry and Vegetative Analysis Studies. Students conducted a study of tree species diversity on a local county park for the Eau Claire County planning office.

Digital Video Production Projects. Students have scripted, filmed, and produced videos for a variety of purposes including tutorials, informational short films, school publicity, and school project video archives. In the past few years students have produced and published on our website over 100 videos on a wide variety of subjects, projects, and tutorial themes.

In addition to our larger, community-connected projects, students work on small group and individual projects to achieve learning goals in math, social studies, English, and other areas of study. Some curricular areas such as math, while still integrated into projects, are approached in a more traditional manner, and students work individually and in small groups focused on the subject at hand. The physical education curriculum revolves around outdoor recreation and lifelong sports. Students participate in canoeing, mountain biking, cross country and downhill skiing, snowshoeing, hiking, backcountry camping, and other outdoor pursuits to earn PE credit.

Students at Wildlands also participate regularly in trips that enhance their learning opportunities. We have visited museums, zoos, civic and governmental operations, as well as outdoor recreation education trips, such as overnight canoeing expeditions and mountain bike trail rides. This is just a sampling of the projects that students have been involved in at Wildlands. Our Lab Bus, driven by staff members (all of whom have a bus driver permit), is essential to the existence of Wildlands as we take our students to new learning opportunities that expand their vision of the world exponentially.

As time went on, we had concerns with documenting and managing student projects. Students (primarily at the high school level) work on a wide variety of projects in diverse subject areas. After a few tries with documentation and management strategies, both created in-house and borrowed, we finally found a very solid and user-friendly project-based learning management system. Project Foundry, headquartered in the Milwaukee area, has been helping schools adapt to project-based learning for many years. After contacting Project Foundry, we set up meetings, in-service sessions, and training time to pilot their computer-based solutions. Project Foundry turned out to be just what Wildlands needed to help the students along the path to independent learning.

At the Core

For many reasons, as we will examine in this book, our students like school. Most, if not all, want to come in every day. The saying

"Teachers make the difference" may be at play here, but we think it's the other way around and say, "Students make the difference." As teachers, we try to make sure they care about the difference they make. What we know: trust and believe in the students, and it is amazing what can happen.

As you will see, much of what we have discovered or, for that matter, rediscovered, is about relationships and how we treat one another at school. Part of our Wildlands core values were eventually developed into the seven essentials for transforming a school. If anything separates us from other schools, it is the core values and seven essentials. They keep our school together, provide common ground, and set the tone for all of our daily interactions. In our view, they are why many families choose this school—and why our school is an extended family. For the rest of this book, we will open the doors to our school and to our students' and teachers' experiences, all framed around the seven essentials, the core of our school culture that has made us successful.

Charter Schools in Wisconsin

There are two types of charter schools in Wisconsin. They are all public schools, but some are affiliated with school districts and others are independently authorized.

An "instrumentality school" is a school district charter school. The charter contract is with a public school district, and a governance board affiliated with the charter operates the school. The contract allows the charter school some flexibility in the way students are served.

Independent charter schools are not affiliated with a public school district and are authorized by a variety of institutions including the city of Milwaukee and universities.

A charter is a contract that defines an agreement between the authorizing body and the school. Every charter contact is different.

Wildlands is a public instrumentality charter school authorized by the School District of Augusta, in Augusta, Wisconsin. Wildlands also has a partnership with our neighboring school district of Fall Creek. Students at the school have to meet the same academic standards and outcomes as any other school. They are assessed like every other student in the public schools and in many ways held to a higher standard because the school's methods are not "traditional." Like all public schools, Wildlands is open to all students who would like to apply. However, every year we get many more applicants than we have space for (the school operates at full capacity) and to be fair, we conduct an enrollment lottery to select new students.

Part II

Transforming School Culture

chapter 3

Essential #1

Relationships

Treat students as people.

At Wildlands, we often hear comments such as "They all seem so busy!" or "How do you get them to behave and work like this?"

The simple truth is we don't GET them to do anything. Instead, we provide an environment with expectations like any other workplace: Treat others as you wish to be treated. Respect everyone and be responsible for yourself and responsible to others—and we will do the same for you. Developing a climate where students feel their needs are number one is a complete flip from other schools they have attended. Being treated as more of an equal in a community is a refreshing change for most students.

Working with students in this way requires developing *real* **relationships** of trust and mutual respect. It involves creating a family atmosphere and developing a good attitude. It requires that we know each other for more than forty-five minutes a day. It requires that we have fun, struggle, have disagreements, solve problems, help each other, and hold each other accountable. It requires that we *all* fall down—adults included—and help each other up. Sometimes, this is literally what happens when a canoe flips or somebody falls into the creek during a project! We are all there to help one another. As teachers, we help students become independent and provide the respectful environment *all* people would like to work in, and we expect high levels of responsibility from students in return.

Our Very Untypical, Typical Day

To develop these relationships between students—and between students and staff—we discovered we had to change the way school days are structured. On a typical day at Wildlands, the high school students all arrive at slightly different times. Some of them drive, some arrive by carpool, and some ride our bus, making for a flexible start time. More often than not, students will arrive, greet staff, have a little social time with their friends while they get set up for the morning's work, and then gather for the Morning Meeting. This is where all of the high school students meet for a few minutes to review the day's big goals, small group meetings, and trips, and go through school event scheduling, updates, and announcements.

After the Morning Meeting, students break into groups or go solo into their first item of work for the day. They all have something on their personal list or perhaps a group project to focus on. Within a few minutes everyone is spread throughout the building, settling in and getting to work. They take breaks when they need to, get up and stretch if they feel like it, and seek out teachers whenever the situation requires it.

Students can schedule meetings with staff, other students, or community mentors, and keep their own calendars. It's not uncommon for a junior or senior to check in with a staff member to ask about taking a meeting with a project contact off site. It can be an amazing experience when a young man or woman comes up and says, "I would like to meet with my veterinarian project mentor next Tuesday at the clinic," or "I have scheduled two days to work with the USGS research team on the Mississippi River next week." We usually respond with, "Sure. Make it a point to follow all our scheduling policies and get your parents in the loop." We all relate to each other in a manner more akin to a business where everyone has a role than a classroom managed by a single teacher.

On days when we are not taking a trip or doing a group project, students are in charge of their day. This can be a lot of responsibility for a ninth grader and even some twelfth graders, but they do it. Some do it better than others, but the ultimate goal is for everyone to move into the independent role of learning to learn, managing their time, accomplishing their own goals, and partnering with the staff to be in charge of their own education. We are proud to say that most of our seniors are staff-members-in-training as they've become so independent and helpful that they are indispensable team members.

Not All Start Out That Way

Students come from such a variety of backgrounds that they each need individualized assistance to develop into a project learner. If a student can't focus, or doesn't have the skills to move forward, our staff helps out; perhaps it is a planning session with the student, or laying out some steps to move toward a goal. This is important especially to the younger students as they adapt to the project world.

One of the most important things we, as teachers, need to keep foremost in our minds and use to guide our interactions, is that **every student has strengths and challenges.** Not one of them is the same, and to treat them that way does not work. They excel in some areas, and they struggle in others. Some things they love, others they don't. How do we help them move toward being a partner with us and fully engaged in their learning? One way is to treat them like individual people instead of a group of students. We want them to be our *partners* in learning, not a bunch of names in our grade books or seating charts.

When it doesn't work—and it doesn't always work—we have to do something about it. The goal is for everyone, students and staff alike, to own all their choices and behaviors. When something goes wrong, or a poor decision is made, we deal with it, learn from it, let it go, and move on. We learn something so we can all do better next time. It is quite simple and very rarely do we have to go beyond a conversation or two. The Wildlands Core Values and the student honor pledge to follow those values are the bottom line, though we can't say it's always perfect. There are absolutes and, as with every public school, violating them can be dire. Violations don't happen very often, but we've had a few issues over the years that have resulted in students having to leave. We have a big advantage in that students *choose* to attend our school. However, students choose for a lot of different reasons, and they come from a wide variety of backgrounds.

Sometimes we hear, "But you get the cream of the crop." Or "Your school skims the best students from other places." But we have no way to do this. As a public school with an open enrollment policy, we offer enrollment to all interested students, regardless of background. We follow federal and state guidelines for non-discrimination and equal access. When students choose to apply to Wildlands, they all go into one big applicant pool. If there are more applicants than spots available, we use a random lottery by grade level. The lottery is held

ecause we always have more applicants than available

eal reason this cosmopolitan grouping of students has so

issues is the way we treat them, include them, trust them,

, work with them, and allow them to be an integral part

...y ...e at school. They know that we are a "want-to- be-there" school and not a "have-to-be-there" school and, of course, that is also an advantage. It would be nice if more students had the opportunity to find schools they *want*. In the final analysis, it is all about relationships, not rules.

Interestingly, a portion of our students who choose to try our school come from situations where a traditional school environment has labeled them as "trouble" or "lazy" etc. Every year we have students who say they didn't like the school they came from. Maybe they were failing. Perhaps they were in a bit of trouble. When they join the Wildlands team, the expectations are clear, mistakes are made, people learn and grow, and we move on.

We have plenty of examples of how different students have gone from "troubled" to "amazing." We can't count the number of times we have heard from other teachers who have worked with our students, "Oh, you will have trouble with that one," or "Watch out." We don't ever put any stock into those comments because our experience tells us it is very often the situation that creates the behaviors. Changing the situation changes the relationships and changes the behaviors. Actually, it became rather simple when we thought of it that way. It's difficult trying to fit somebody into an inflexible situation, the square-peg round-hole game. Once we realized we needed a square hole and some flexibility, it got easier.

Many of our students have been categorized in some way with attention deficit or hyperactivity issues. In some cases, these are very real behavioral issues, but it is not our role to judge or classify. However, the environment in which we deal with them is so very important. For many students, making them sit all day means asking for trouble. When we involve them, give them some flexibility, let them move, support their goals, and even provide more physical outlets, we can see positive changes. We *like* the active students; they keep us moving, they challenge us as a staff, and they can be some of the best "doers" we know. It is all about understanding them, developing a true relationships with them, and helping them find ways to be their best instead of fitting them into some predetermined mold.

Teambuilding

The focus of the first few weeks of school is always on the student, our community, and building positive relationships. We engage students in challenges, both academically and physically. We focus on working with them, helping them define their goals for the year, setting goals for the school, and developing plans to get there. The students are involved in activities ranging from outdoor training, canoe and water safety, bike trips visiting unique natural areas, overnight team building and confidence trips, to large group projects focusing on any subject matter. The key is building cohesiveness of relationships among all members of our community and to learn to rely on one another, work together, play together, and learn together. To do this effectively, teambuilding is vital.

Our middle school spends a good portion of the first month in teambuilding activities. The thematic multidisciplinary units that weave throughout the year accommodate a wide variety of team-oriented activities. These help to create the sense of shared responsibility, the single purpose of the group, and build working relationships among students and also with our staff.

The high school students continue this journey as they participate in the early activities of the fall. One very interesting and important element of challenging the students early in the year is to put them in situations where they have to adapt, use their strengths, and show leadership or good team member behavior. There is no coasting and no hiding; everyone is involved. In many cases they have to demonstrate abilities outside the typical academic realms. By doing this they are creating roles for themselves within the group, they are developing relationships with their peers and the staff, and everyone has the opportunity to be a valued member of the community.

Parent Relationships

To establish similar levels of communication and trust with our parents, we work with them in a number of ways. Before school starts we host orientation meetings for new and returning families. We have an often-repeated "open door" policy where parents are encouraged to stop in anytime they can. We also schedule our student/parent conferences so everyone has a chance and is invited to attend. Emails, phone calls, and letters all add to the mix of communications with parents. Even video meetings and access to video presentations students make are available. Sometimes the staff jokes about being "communication officers" because we often are in touch with many parents in a given day. In our opinion that is great! We *want* them to be a part of our family, and we want to develop solid relationships with them as they support their child's learning.

It is amazing when, year after year, parents come to us worried about how many openings the school will have for the next fall. Siblings of current students are our most consistent enrollment pool and parents of current students are also our best advertisement for recruiting new students. Word of mouth and the grapevine are the primary ways families hear about Wildlands. The relationships we have built with families of both current and former students have carried the school far in both the public relations and enrollment categories.

Community Relationships

Over the years we have teamed up with a wide variety of individuals, groups, businesses, and government agencies on projects. These have been anything from a day or two on a specific project, to a year and a half long study that culminated with meetings, reports, publications, and next step plans. Developing relationships with what we like to call a *Mentor* or *Partner Network* is especially important in helping put our students in the context of learning outside the school building.

Whether it is developing habitats for amphibians with the Natural Resource Conservation Service, mapping a local lake, interviewing people and documenting first person history, conducting water quality studies, or doing wildlife research, if the outcome is a shared project where others outside of our school depend on us, it adds relevance and builds substantial relationships with partners.

It is common for people and organizations to contact us with ideas for projects our students could carry out. Most of these ideas have tremendous merit in the academic sense as well as the real-world outcome. If the projects fit the goals of the students, we take them on. Other times we need to modify the ideas, and sometimes we have to thank them but decline due to time factors, relevance, or student needs. We feel honored when people contact the school to see if our students would like to be involved in research, development, or other types of projects. This shows that the variety of relationships we are building with our community are valued and necessary.

Trust and Transparency

In order to be a viable small school with a teacher-powered management and decision-making model, we have to have an open and positive relationship with the administration and school board of Augusta, our sponsoring district. Since the first year, we have maintained an open line of communication and worked to meet the community goals set by both our school and the school district. The key to maintaining the positive nature of this partnership is to have systems in place that allow for 100 percent transparency in matters of budget, staffing, scheduling, student management, and school goals. Accountability goes right along with transparency.

As a teacher-powered school, we have to be first and foremost accountable to our students and families. As a public school, we also have to be accountable to all the levels of management from the local district to the state and beyond. This creates a situation where our teacher team wears many hats and does much more than the typical teacher job. Over the years as the teacher-powered model has developed, the trust factor has been critical for our success as a school. Without it we could not have evolved into the school we are today. To live up to the trust extended to our team, we have to make sure things are done right, we have to be on top of the day-to-day management, deliver on goals, maintain open and regular communications, and share information whenever necessary. It is beyond the scope of this book to really dig into the factors we feel are critical in a teacher-managed school, but we will delve into this topic more in Book Two of this series.

A teacher-powered school that is managed with few staff members is indeed a challenge. Within that challenge is the need to have dynamic and positive working relationships among the adults in the building. When everything required to operate the school is in the realm of a few teachers as a management co-op, it can get quite busy and sometimes chaotic. The way to navigate through the busyness and chaos is to know we are not alone and that we have fully functional partners and can work as a team. The teachers need the teambuilding

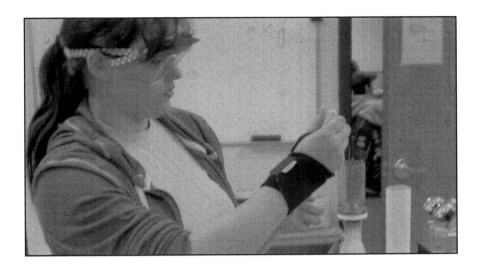

and relationship activities as much as the students do. That is why we participate with our students in nearly all of our activities and projects. We either lead, advise, or become a worker bee right next to the kids. We do the same high ropes challenges, unswamp the canoes and do deep-water rescues, help with research, assist in the design of project methods and timelines, and sometimes just become a student again.

As a group we get to know each other's strengths and challenges. Somehow, everyone naturally migrates to responsibilities in areas where they excel and fit them as a professional and, in areas where we need someone to help, we aren't afraid to ask. Oftentimes we have to stretch our own limits and work in areas we are not 100 percent comfortable with, which is good for us, too. When that happens, we reach out just like our students would. We find experts and mentors, and we build our skill sets to get the job done. It is a climate of mutual respect, shared responsibility, shared decision making, and continuous improvement. This is necessary because at the end of each day we are fully responsible for everything that makes our school. Staff that facilitates a *buck stops here* and *get it done* attitude, connections with students and parents that allow their full participation, and the development of community are advantages our school couldn't do without.

Mixed Messages

At Wildlands, students and teachers are in it together. We work together. We play together. Students see staff as there to help, lend a hand, and listen. It is often the opposite in a regular school. Students saw the adults as *them*, the ones who are in charge, the rule makers, the givers of knowledge and assignments, but also detentions and punishments.

Earlier in my career when I was at traditional school, I remember a faculty meeting during which a principal told the teachers to make sure they were in the hall between classes during passing time. This would cut down on the monkey business, running, goofing off, bullying, and the like. Then, he said to make sure we stood at our doors and greeted students as they came into our rooms and to take time to learn all the names right away so the students felt at home. The next item on the agenda was the new detention policies, and a stack of detention slip packets were handed around with the comment to make sure we sent the copies of each violation to the office.

Talk about mixed messages! In the hall we were behavior monitors, at the door we were greeters and make-them-feel-at-home agents; then we had to remember to be the law enforcement agents with our nice, little, yellow detention slips. It is no wonder few real trusting and beneficial relationships between students and staff develop very often in most traditional schools. Sure, many teachers get to know their students, but it is difficult to develop quality relationships around learning and personal growth when the teachers are also the police force.

As we developed Wildlands, we tried to fold behavioral and rule management issues into the culture of day-to-day student life. We worked to make the students part of every plan and many decisions. We didn't want the school where a supervisor has to tell teachers to greet students as a policy issue, or to watch them, or hand out detentions, etc. We wanted a school where we could work with all students, assist them, and build the kind of relationships where trust and mutual assistance in all aspects of school life were paramount.

How about a T-shirt?

To have a school where students are involved in their own learning path, work through projects, plan, suggest, create, and control the culture, it is necessary to have a place where relationships between all the people in the school are positive, mature, and nurturing. Developing these kinds of relationships makes it much easier to work with them in the more difficult academic areas later in the year. The communication lines are open, the honesty established, and the trust is there.

Here again our staff sets the tone. We had to quit looking at students as vessels for us to pour knowledge into or as children in need of our expertise. We admit we don't know it all and learn right along with the students. Real conversations are vital, especially ones centering on the student, who they are, what they need, and how they see themselves as learners.

Conversations and common experiences are the essence of establishing a solid culture and positive relationships. Removing the walls of traditional sit-and-get culture is not so hard if the focus shifts to creating common experiences that add challenge, cultivate meaningful relationships, and provide creative outlets for the students.

The students are children, but they are people, too. Our staff has a little inside slogan: *Wildlands School: treating students like people since 2005.* Maybe we need a billboard, or at least a T-shirt.

chapter 4

Essential #2

Values

We all act like decent human beings.

In our first year at Wildlands, we realized we were on a path that few had traveled. A list of rules saying *no chewing gum, raise your hand if you want to speak,* and *you need a pass to use the bathroom* didn't seem to fit the environment we wanted to create. We needed something different because our situation was so different. Therefore, we did something that doesn't seem to happen very often: we asked the students what *they* wanted.

In 2005, on a beautiful fall day with a slight breeze and lots of sunshine, a group of twenty high school students sat on picnic tables. These students were part of the first group of students to walk through the doors of Wildlands Science Research Charter School. Each had come with a different skill set from different school districts and, as juniors and seniors in high school, they were all looking for something new and different in their educational careers. They were there to do projects and get out into the fields, lakes, rivers, and forests. They didn't really know what to expect, but they knew being a student at Wildlands would be different.

As the staff and students began to talk about what we wanted our "new school" to be like, the subjects of rules, handbooks, student behavior, and discipline were discussed. At one point, an insightful student spoke up with questions and comments regarding rules. "I don't think we need rules," he said. "We've been told rules our entire lives. Society has rules we all follow. Why don't we all just behave like humans who know right from wrong? Why don't we just act as if we were in the real world, instead of trapped in some school that acts like a Big Brother or jail?"

The staff responded with more questions: "How do we do that?" "How do we change the way we, as adults, behave so students feel responsible and empowered to be in control—and accountable for that control?" The important part here is this: **the staff was *asking*, not telling.** This dialogue led to a discussion of what it is to be a good person, a team player, and a productive, functioning member of a community with shared goals and values.

Most of these Wildlands pioneers brought up the idea that high school was a bit of a game when it came to behaviors and rules. Kids learned to play it, one way or another. If you didn't want to follow all the rules—or a certain teacher's behavior system—you learned to play behind the scenes, bend the rules, get away with things, or fly under the radar. The more rules, the more the game-like atmosphere. If you got caught not following some rule, different teachers had different interpretations of the consequences. A lot of times it was all about learning which teachers were the enforcers and which were not. Many times, it felt like a jail with little freedom: Do what you are told. If you break a rule there will be penalties like extra school work, sitting in quiet rooms, no talking, no moving, no anything. Somebody will be there to enforce that you pay the price and sit your time. And don't forget you are expected to do "schoolwork" during those penalty box times, those detention sessions.

One of the students pointed out how absolutely silly and absurd it was to use schoolwork and learning as a penalty. "Wow," she said, "teachers want people to learn and maybe enjoy things such as reading or writing, yet they use them as a *punishment?*" She commented on how the PA system announcements used to really make her laugh. "Detention will be at 3:20 pm. Bring schoolwork or something to read."

Soon the question came up: *How in the world did schools get this way?* These twenty students had hit a huge bunch of essential questions: Why do we treat students this way? Why can't schools be more like life? More like real experiences and with real human interaction? Mistakes coupled with learning? A place to learn from mistakes—and bounce back—instead of a jail or discipline colony?

One of the students commented that he thought schools and their rules were built around the premise that all children were bad and need to be corrected, coerced, and modified. That kids couldn't be trusted. (*Wow. These young people were unearthing some pretty fundamental ideas of how some schools treat students.*) A comment was also made to the effect of, "If you go along, you'll get along, but you're just giving in and being like all the other sheep. Watch out if you try to express your freedom or individual interests." (Obviously this student had some experience with coloring outside the lines.) Another point was tossed out that schools have to be this way because they are handling so many students at the same time. Many kids don't want to be there or don't like a subject and they cause trouble, which screws it up for the rest. All the students agreed that was a good thing not to let the fools and clowns run the show, but they also thought it was too bad everyone paid the price for a few who didn't care.

Since the start of this conversation, one young man had been fairly quiet. He'd told us earlier he had decided to come to Wildlands because it didn't seem it would be like regular school where he was bored out of his mind. He didn't go to school often and sometimes was considered truant during his first two years of high school. When we asked him why, he said two things really bugged him. One, teachers made him do things that he already knew over and over and that bored him. Two, he felt he was always the one being controlled, managed, and not trusted—and he didn't like that. He preferred to have some say. At this point in the conversation, he spoke up. He asked, "Why couldn't a school be like a workplace? Why can't students be expected to be part of the operation? Be trusted? Be treated more like adults, especially in high school where kids are getting very close to *being* adults." He asked, "Why is it that everywhere else in society, people, kids included, know mostly how to behave, but schools have to have these laundry lists of do and don't things that are all about control?"

At this point the teachers in the meeting responded. "What would happen if a school just asked the students to act like decent human beings, and what does that mean?" The response was overwhelming. RIGHT! **Act like humans and be treated like humans.** We all know the rules; we know about societies' laws and regulations. We all know what is socially acceptable in public places like schools, stores, and the like. Why can't we be expected to behave like everyone else and not have a ton of minuscule rules that change from one teacher to the next? We responded to those students' questions with a very simple idea: **YOU CAN.** Perhaps we need to figure out what it means to be trusted and act like an adult. What are those things you are talking about that "everyone knows"? How do we grapple with the ideas of behavior if we have no rules, and then what happens when someone is out of line? Immediately the students said, "Tell them to fix it—or leave." If somebody can't be a part of the group, a part of the team, and decides to act in a way that messes it up for everyone else, then that person shouldn't be here. Because this wasn't *regular school,* and nobody was forced to be there, they felt they had some room to stretch out and try their ideas on for size.

It wasn't long before they were putting together lists, ideas, topics, and debating each other about the value of their notions. As we sat back, watched, and listened, it occurred to us it might be time to present these kids with an idea. We stood up from the picnic table after quietly discussing our plan and asked the students to listen for a second. We challenged them to come up with a list of attributes or characteristics they felt made up this *everybody knows how to act* idea. Try to isolate and put into words the core of how people should be in a school or workplace, or even everyday life. Then, once they had the list, to think about how we could use such a list. We then left them to work as a team, and the only instruction was to get us when they were ready to share what they had come up with.

As we watched from a distance, one of the things that impressed us right away about this group was that they immediately were able to discuss as a team. They weren't perfect, but it was evident these kids wanted to be here, and they wanted to be part of how this school culture was developed. After a while, we were summoned back to the picnic tables. One young lady took the lead and began reading the list to us:

With each item she read on the list, the students began adding clarifying thoughts. They felt it was necessary to explain more

- **Honesty**
- **Personal responsibility**
- **Self-respect**
- **Respecting others**
- **Care and respect of school property**
- **Trust**
- **Service**
- **Punctuality**
- **Attendance**
- **Courtesy**
- **Effort**
- **Independence**
- **Team work**
- **Accountability**
- **Participation**
- **Quality**
- **Job done right**
- **Pride**
- **Being a positive member of our family/community**

about *why* each of the characteristics on their list was chosen. There was no real priority order to the list; they wanted each idea to have somewhat equal weight and be just as important on its own as well as how it related to the others. For example, they felt *honesty* was something that could be found in all the other characteristics, yet it needed to be on the list because without it we would need to have *rules*. If the school were to run so that the students were part of the plan, then they had to be responsible both to themselves and others. At the end they asked us what we thought about the list. This exercise in group thinking impressed us so much, and they had such compelling reasons for including each trait, all we could respond with was a single question: what do we call this list of characteristics?

Many ideas for a formal name flew around the group. The idea of rules was quickly thrown out. These weren't rules. They were attributes or characteristics. These were things to aspire to, ways to see their role in the group and at the school. The name of the list probably didn't really matter, one student replied. Others said it did, and we had to have a name that would stick. A name that would represent what we as a group felt was important if the school were to run in such a way that we all were expected to act "like humans" who know how to behave in a workplace. One student suggested these were not just characteristics: they were more like *values*, ways of being. That led to a discussion of how the ideas on this list should represent the *core* of how students should behave at Wildlands. It didn't take long to put the two together, and the students decided we should call this list *Wildlands Core Values*. Ever since, the core values have been a centerpiece of our school.

Students revisit our core values in many ways through various activities and on all of our trips. They have become the cornerstone of who we are as a school community and what our students and staff represent. The older students take pride in sharing and explaining what it really means to be a Wildlands student and exhibit the core values on a daily basis, even when people aren't watching. Every time our students embark on a trip, a visit, or any project or service outside our school, we ask them a simple question: whom do you represent? Through our discussions they have come to understand they represent themselves, their families, and our school. It's become a matter of pride and a constant reminder that they are judged by the outside world not by their intelligence or intent, but by how they act, how people see them. We want people to see them just as we do: as amazing humans.

An unplanned demonstration of the power of these values as part of our school culture happened as a result of our students' reaction to an immense national tragedy in 2012. I vividly remember the evening of Friday, December 14, 2012, watching the breaking-news reports of the Sandy Hook Elementary shooting being covered by different media stations. I tried hard to blink away tears as I listened to horrifying details and watched gut-wrenching images of frightened little kids plastered on the big screen in front of me. I looked over at my little boys, one and three years old, and thought, "School shootings are becoming way too common." My kids (I include my students, too) are growing up in a world where too many headlines are bad news. I just felt numb.

The following Monday evening a reporter from NBC News shared a story on a movement called The 26 Acts of Kindness, intended to honor the victims of Newtown, Connecticut, and wondered if people would join in and complete their own. People across the country were posting pictures of letters and money they had left for strangers, pictures of extra large tips left to their servers, notes explaining that they bought the coffee for the cars behind them in the drive-thru, and so on.

Tuesday, during Morning Meeting, the staff gave our list of usual announcements, and then I had one more: I challenged the students to be a part of the #26Acts movement. Plan and complete twenty-six acts of kindness as a school by the end of the school year. Immediately following the meeting, buzz about what could be done for twenty-six acts took off as fast as hugs among the group were given out. News of this adventure went home, and students came back to school with monetary donations from their parents to help us get any supplies we needed to make these acts possible. In the end over $800 was collected, and it all went to some sort of act of kindness. The generosity and pride of being a part of this project was carrying over from our students to their families and into the greater community. Students could already tell they were making a difference.

Each event was coordinated by a student or a small group of students, but had lots of participation from the rest of the group. Students read to local elementary students, visited the local nursing home, made blankets for those in need, made and served lunch with an organization that feeds anyone and everyone a free meal once a day, sent six enormous care packages to US troops stationed in Afghanistan, shoveled random driveways and sidewalks after a big snowstorm, and picked up trash at a rest stop while on a field trip. These kids were living and breathing the Wildlands Core Values through projects with incredible meaning for each of them and our community.

After the twenty-six acts were completed, students began to realize it was not about a number. The number was meaningful, and it honored the victims of that terrible school tragedy, but it seemed to be a number that implied an end point. Students began suggesting new and different service projects we could get involved in because they knew they weren't done serving others. This was a start, not an end. Since those initial twenty-six acts of kindness, our school and students have developed a service-learning appetite they are always trying to satisfy. The students love it, the staff supports it, and it provides meaning, relevance, context, and connection to every student's learning.

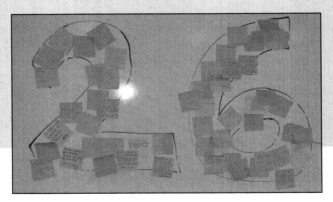

We Are All In This Together

The list of core values appears in the student handbook, is featured in one of our YouTube videos, and permeates all that we do as students and staff to maintain a healthy, mature, and responsive learning environment. This learning environment values each individual and their role in the community. To be a Wildlands student, a young person must agree to work hard at maintaining these values, and they sign an honor pledge to that effect. To successfully operate a school where students are participating in the planning and development of much of their learning, they also have to be in control of themselves, their behavior, and their choices. As a school, we visit and revisit our core values throughout the year in both purposeful activities and by applying them during learning reflection and debriefing meetings.

Sometimes people will ask us, "Why spend so much time and energy on these 'non-content' areas?" The answer is simple: we believe that values shape culture. When we realized how powerful the environment and the culture of the school was for shaping attitudes toward learning and work habits, we opted for investing time and energy into creating that positive environment and culture. When those things work, so do students—and so does the school. We provide students with roles within the school culture and the operation of the school where they are trusted, depended upon, and valued. We will say it again: **values shape the culture.** If a school simply values rules, structure, content, grades, and tests, then it becomes a rules, structure, content, grades, and test culture. If a school values the students first and provides the context for developing a positive learning culture, it can make a major difference in how students view learning. Learning in the traditional "tested" content areas becomes a much smoother and a more successful venture and, in some ways, almost an artifact of a positive learning environment. In a values-based culture, teachers can do their jobs, students can do theirs—and everyone is in it *together*.

chapter 5

Essential #3

Opportunity

Put students first and allow them the opportunity to make decisions regarding their education.

In a traditional school, students are rarely presented with opportunities to make the final decision or any decision related to their learning—especially in the classroom. Their class schedule is produced out of an obscure matrix of graduation expectations and open seats. Specifications regarding daily assignments are spelled out for each class by individual teachers (makes for easier grading, right?), and a bell usually rings to tell them it's time to move on to the next "opportunity." At Wildlands, we make it clear to students that when they walk into our building they are entering a world of *real* opportunity. They get to decide what to take advantage of—and we support them.

Let's pretend, for fun, we were creating a lesson plan for every student's educational career. If we had to write out a list of objectives that each student deserves to meet regarding opportunities, this would be our list:

Students should have the opportunity to . . .

- learn in an environment that suits their learning style, personality, and personal strengths

- develop a voice in their own learning; recognize strengths and areas of need, act on them, and reflect on their personal progress

- be part of a cooperative team that manages their learning and learn to plan their path in school

- work with adults who recognize every learner is different, has unique abilities, and can act accordingly to develop educational opportunities tailored to student learning

- be challenged, held accountable, and own their decisions about how and what they do in school

- participate in a school culture that values every student, fosters independence, and develops skills for lifelong learning

- attend a school where they not only want to be, but also where they feel incredibly connected to the school, the staff, and the culture of the organization

- contribute to meaningful activities that have connections to the school, local community, and even regional or national issues

- have meaningful conversations with adults about more than content and grades

- have a voice in everyday school decisions that affect them

- be in situations daily where their choices matter, and they can learn to be their own time manager, set personal goals, and be the first check of quality learning and work

These *opportunity* statements develop a learning culture where students are truly embedded in the full learning process. For years teachers have been the planners, the implementors, and the directors of the learning. Most teachers have followed rigid pre-planned curriculum. It's their job, right? However, in order to flip this system and have students in charge of their own learning, something has to give—to change. Without a doubt, if we could give teachers one piece of advice, we would recommend they **let the students teach them.** Students have a great deal to offer if they are provided the opportunity. Opportunity can present itself anywhere, anyplace, anytime. It is all about being open to the experience, looking at what presents itself, and learning from it.

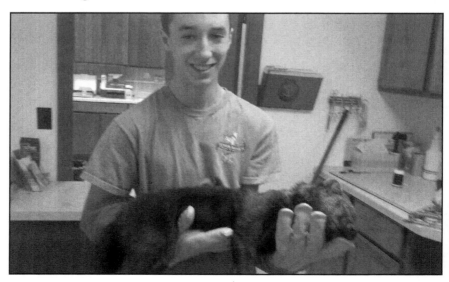

Ah-Ha

During the 1990s I was fortunate to develop a summer science research program at a traditional middle and high school in partnership with a few colleagues. Teachers recruited students from grades 7–12 to work on research projects with local resource partners such as the Wisconsin Department of Natural Resources (WDNR) and the Eau Claire County Land Conservation Department.

Throughout the summer, students gathered the background resources, defined the questions, learned and summarized the field and lab methods, developed quality assurance processes for the investigations, collected, processed, and analyzed the data. Sure, we as teachers helped along the side, assisted in gathering needed resources, and provided transportation, but the students were the real drivers. Reports and presentations were given to the partner organizations, both in person and in written form. Discussions of their findings were conducted with the professionals and interested community organizations as if the students had been employed in the field for years. Bottom line: students were able to participate in authentic, firsthand learning, an active team-oriented project, and they experienced a sense of success and value that wouldn't have been found within the classroom walls.

Each summer presented different questions, projects, and activities, but one thing remained constant: **I was astounded by the involvement and performance of each student, from all ability levels.** It didn't matter if they were typical high achievers or disinterested classroom students who needed remedial credits from summer school; everyone performed as a team, experienced success when they were involved, and knew they had choice and some control in their role while they worked on meaningful, relevant projects that impacted our community. Everyone on the team was a valued person.

DING! There is that little lightbulb going off in my head.

Why don't we have more school experiences that imitate this summer science program? How come these are "special" experiences that only a few students get to be involved in? These students demonstrated to me year after year that they were all capable, trustworthy individuals. They didn't need to be programmed and follow canned lessons. They could be part of effective problem-solving teams. These young people could be partners in learning and doing, instead of just recipients of my lesson plans. There wasn't any worry about grades or assignments because, in the summer projects, students had to be responsible to each other and work as professional teams with a collective purpose that answered to others outside of our school.

This was as much of a different role for them as it was for me. Instead of being looked to as the content expert, judge, jury, and evaluator, I was now part of the team. Of course I remained the adult, but **I was welcomed by the students to learn side by side with them.** Assuming the role of advisor, guide, resource person, and manager of the project was a turning point, changing what I believed my role as a teacher was supposed to be.

This summer program led to an enormous shift in perspective. Some may call it a paradigm shift. Whatever it was, the power of students came through loud and clear. They were saying trust us. We can do it. Stop treating us like we are in need of total adult control. Let us drive. Let us learn from failure and pick ourselves up. It was the first baby step toward developing Wildlands as we know it today. The best lessons I have ever learned about teaching have been from students. I just had to keep my eyes open and let them show me the way.

Projects and More

Our vision of creating a "Learning Community Based in the Natural World" has its roots in learning through meaningful community-connected projects with students primarily in the driver's seat. A new choice. A different opportunity. **Not the same stuff they do in other schools.** We changed the roles of students and teachers, changed our focus from curriculum, classroom management, discipline, and planning, to a focus on the students and providing them with opportunities. To build this learning community, we chose to use the project-based learning (PBL) focus, not as the only way to learn, but as the centerpiece of a variety of learning alternatives students can utilize.

The key to understanding PBL is understanding teacher and student roles or responsibilities for the projects—the planning, learning, accomplishments, and evaluation. To embrace PBL, the culture of the school needs to shift. The ultimate goal is for the *student* to determine the goals, methods, outcome, quality, and accomplishment. The student is working toward personal control in choosing the path to fulfill both requirements and elective areas of study. If the student can become his or her own best critic, know how to check for accuracy and quality, and have an ethic of getting things done right—even if they have to be done over—then we are on the right track.

Project-based learning can come in many forms, like brands in the marketplace. You can choose a Chrysler 300 or a Ford Focus. Both get you from here to there, but have very different features, design, and mileage. Some people like Chrysler better than Ford or Ford more than Chevy. (Probably should stop this train of thought as it can lead to pickup truck window stickers of little boys urinating on brand logos, but the point is valid.) People like different features, have different preferences, and want choices.

Why should education be any different?

When it comes to PBL, there is no cookie cutter answer. Some schools are structured PBL, some are inquiry-based, some have rigid standardized templates for projects, others have student-designed programs and processes, and so on. At Wildlands, we have several types of PBL happening at the same time. We have learned—sometimes the hard way—that PBL in itself is not a big solution to all learning or educational issues. It is a tool that can be used. The tool has some great advantages when students are given the opportunity and become partners in learning.

Wildlands has built a school where students can provide *themselves* with more and more control of their own destinies through the development and demonstration of skills, knowledge, abilities, and in many cases maturity. Within that system are support mechanisms to help all the students reach a point of pure independence and intrinsic motivation by the time they are seniors. We have developed our own types of PBL and the tools to accompany them to fit the needs of the students we have.

Let's take a look at what we consider to be the three general categories of PBL in our school: teacher-led PBL, guided PBL, and independent PBL. (By the way, we don't use these categories as measuring sticks or even do any formal discussions with the students about them. These are simply the ways we mark our students' progress along the path to becoming an independent, lifelong learner.)

Typically, teacher-led PBL is an introduction to the processes of project learning. Guided PBL generally applies to younger or newer students, with independent PBL the ultimate goal for all students. (Keep in mind these categories are not cast in stone and have a wide range of flexibility among them. Sometimes students have personal attributes that coincide with independent PBL at much younger ages, but also need some teacher-led activities.)

Teacher-Led PBL

Teacher-led PBL is the most basic kind of PBL and is best suited for most of the middle school students, or those with little to no experience in a project-learning environment. It is more of a teacher-directed, planned, and guided level. At our school, we integrate teacher-directed PBL into the middle school, and it is designed to support and train students in PBL. In the middle school grades, the projects are built around thematic units. The teacher plans, organizes, and sets goals and timelines for the investigations or projects. The students work in the theme area and will produce projects as a whole class, groups, small teams, and individually. Each theme is a multidisciplinary look at a big topic or question. Within each theme, students will be working in science, math, history, the arts, and other curricular areas concurrently as part of the objectives for that particular unit. That said, Teacher-Led PBL is not exclusive to the middle school level and can be used at *any time* to train new students, reinforce skills, or even work in larger groups on central themes.

Students in a teacher-led PBL environment have some choice in how they approach projects within these areas, and they also have some specific requirements. Requirements are set forth by coordinating the area of project work with the outcomes desired based on target skills and standards. As the students move through teacher-led projects, they become more and more acclimated to what is expected of an independent learner. Because those middle-school years are really the training ground for our high school, the students learn many of the basic skills of independence, time management, teamwork, community role, and work ethic.

The teacher helps make sure the content is integrated, the subjects are explored, and the projects are coordinated. Then the students have choices within those projects to design the research and explorations they are interested in, while meeting all the requirements. The *Teacher makes the difference* saying holds very true for the middle school age students and helping develop the basic skills needed for project-based learning. Without strong leadership, organization, and purposeful activities and investigations, the students won't gain confidence in their abilities to do their own projects.

Guided PBL

Guided PBL is a bridge between the more structured teacher-directed environment of the middle school and early project learners, and the independent learner PBL environment that all students should strive for. Guided PBL offers students some teacher direction and more specific learning plans but requires students to be a bit more independent, self-motivated, and responsible for completing tasks. Some students shoot through this level quickly and become full PBL participants easily. Others need more help and guidance. Typically ninth and tenth grade students need this type of support anywhere from nine weeks to nine months. We realize this is a very broad generalization, and students develop PBL skills at an individual pace. We don't expect them to pick up all of the necessary skills right out of the gate.

If a high school student joins the Wildlands team and has not been in our middle school program, it can be a bit more difficult to adapt to PBL. This second level of PBL development is designed for students at *any* age, dependent on their PBL skill levels. If students come to us from other more traditional schools, we literally have to help the parents and students understand that there is a period of "unlearning" the habits and patterns they have been used to for a long time. Students who join us with between eight and eleven years of traditional school background where they have been told exactly what to do, what to learn, when to do it, and tested only on what they can remember on a test, can be a little intimidated or lost in the world of projects. They have a steep learning curve to accomplish as they work toward becoming an independent project-based learner.

Sometimes we joke with the students about the old *Is this good enough?* or *What do you want me to do?*mentality. We have to be somewhat gentle and very mindful as we help them out of the old ways and into the new world of "YOU are in charge of your learning." "YOU are your own best measure of quality." "YOU are done when you know it is done right, and done well, and demonstrates your learning." It can be very difficult for some students, as they have always looked to the teachers or other adults for validation of their learning and accomplishments. How do we know when it's working? One indicator is when students begin to stand up for themselves, argue with us a little and defend their work, and ask to be assessed or evaluated because they want feedback on their work. Key phrase here is *they want*. The early years of high school at Wildlands are designed to help move students toward more independent thinking and learning behaviors.

Independent PBL

Independent PBL is nearing the mastery level of PBL. Students who work on projects and demonstrate this level of understanding have habits of mind associated with internal motivation and are *in control* of their learning plan. They are very highly functioning individuals in our school. These students typically help others move up the rungs of the ladder toward learning independence and are key players in the culture and day-to-day operation of the school. Regardless of age, once a student makes the transition to true self-determined PBL, we feel they have acquired a set of personal skills and characteristics any employer, school, university, or branch of the military will value. Remember Molly's graduation speech at the beginning of the book?

Students in the early high school grades have more specific learning plans (goals and standards) to meet, because they need to demonstrate proficiency and mastery of certain basic skills and earn credit in required areas for graduation. Thus, there are group study topics, seminars, projects, and team investigations designed to help the students move through these areas. Some students choose to join the groups and take advantage of more teacher-student partnership planning, and others attack their learning plan more independently.

This is where knowing our students and understanding their personal areas of strength and challenges is key. To do that, we have to spend time talking with the students about some of the key factors of success in our school. Not just the things they need to know, or the content they need to cover, but the attitudes, habits, and skills that will help determine their success. However, in most cases if a student isn't fitting into the PBL mode by the end of ninth grade, perhaps it isn't the best way for that particular child to learn. Occasionally, we have to cross that bridge and work with parents to really make sure the student's needs are met, even if it means other school options.

Somebody Has to Own It

At this point it might be interesting to note that we have not yet spoken much about the "content" of the learning in our school. We do have projects posted on our website, as well as almost 100 videos of projects and other related topics on our video page. Visit **www.wildlandschool.net** to check them out.

We use the same standards and learning targets as other schools in our state, but we fold them into a completely different learning culture. Our goal is to focus on the students as people and to help them become their best. The content is learned as a by-product of the process. We want to provide students opportunities to really dig into projects and be owners of their learning. Kind of backwards from the way most schools see it. We know that, but as you will see when we discuss how Wildlands students do on those highly publicized standardized tests (Chapter 10, "How's It Going?"), you will see **our students have been achieving at or above the levels of the state averages and other area school districts.** We think this is because we always come back to one of our real central questions: Do we want quality people who can do what they set their minds to, enjoy learning, and go for their goals? Or do we just want good test takers? Funny thing is, we see both.

When students have been at Wildlands for a while, they typically develop abilities that allow them to fully partner with the staff in the learning process. There really isn't a magic system that allows us as staff to "get them there." It happens most often when they realize nobody is going to do it for them. The opportunity is there. Most grab it and run after a period of acclimation. When young people realize that they can fulfill requirements pursuing areas they are interested in, it changes their perspective.

Writing about their fishing adventure or the skateboard they built with Grandpa, or reading books and articles that interest them to dissect for English skill development, tends to remove some innate hesitation some kids have about doing schoolwork. They become invested in their own school experience. Doing a health project by interviewing various health professionals and writing it up for both health and English credit is far more engaging than reading a chapter on health professions and turning in those ten questions at the end. Turning a passion for cooking into a science project or spending every Tuesday with a veterinarian in surgery becomes gratifying and meaningful.

What happens is the student is now steering the ship, following dreams and ideas, working hand in hand with staff to define projects, gathering resources, planning processes, and recruiting outside experts and mentors, and they are learning by doing meaningful work. In most cases we strive for those projects and that work to be connected to our local or regional community. We push for service components, outside experiences, use of local community resources, and people. We make it so doing it right, learning all that is required, and reporting on outcome has some real-life stakes attached. Make it matter. Failure is not an option. Do-over's are encouraged. Due dates still apply. Don't just make it an assignment, make it an opportunity, because opportunity can be found anytime, anywhere, and anyplace if you look for it.

chapter 6

Essential #4

Adventure

Adventure = Learning by doing, being involved, and taking initiative

Flames leapt fifty feet in the air, forming a tight vortex of orange and yellow waves dancing against the bright blue sky. Suddenly, the smoke formed a corkscrew pattern extending a couple hundred feet into the air and drifted off with the slight wind. "Fire tornado," explained the restoration biologist who'd arranged the prairie burn for the students. "When the heat gets so intense and the grasses are all burning so fiercely, it creates that spiral vortex for a couple moments, like a tornado of fire. Not something you see every day," he continued. Together, we marveled at the sight, but soon everyone's attention turned back to the fire and keeping the edges of the burn under control.

Students were spread over the prairie, holding rakes, shovels, and damping tools. A few were wearing water pump backpacks so they could get to any spreading flames quickly. The area wasn't that large, but the thick, dry grass from the previous season's growth provided quite a show of heat, flames, and smoke. It was all over in a matter of a few minutes.

After the flames subsided, the group carried out the tasks assigned to them by the biologist, making sure the burn was completely out and it was safe to leave. Then the discussion continued on the edge of the blackened prairie for quite some time, picking up on our previous discussions at school about why we burn prairies. We talked about prairie plants and their fire adaptations, their deep roots, the role of fire in ecosystem development, and the history of the American prairie ecosystem. We talked about what it must've been like to see massive walls of prairie fires rolling across the midwestern landscapes in pre-settlement times. Science, history, ecosystem management, and restoration ecology all folded into one adventure. Still, as far as some of the students were concerned, the fire tornado was the ultimate prize. Not a typical day at most schools, but not out of the ordinary at Wildlands.

What Did You Do Today?

"What did you do at school today?" is a phrase that's been heard in households for generations. Unfortunately, the answer's often, "Not much." Or even worse: "Nothing." How rare is the answer,

"We burned a prairie," accompanied by an explanation about how—and why. Or, "We built a biological scavenger hunt on the reserve." Or, "We designed a soil analysis project to help figure out where to restore a wetland on some farmlands, and tomorrow we're collecting soil samples."

School = Adventure = FUN?

Hmmm. The classroom learning most of us remember wasn't often viewed as fun, and probably never viewed as an adventure. But why not? Perhaps it's because there are no standards for adventure, and no benchmarks or rubrics to evaluate student performance. How in the world do you give a test on adventure? It could be that adventures are hard to pack into small blocks of time and stop every time a bell rings. Adventures can't be ordered from suppliers and curriculum companies. Maybe they demand too much forethought and are too troublesome to create. Really? Again, we ask, why?

Adventure is what keeps people coming back for more. Adventure can hook you and draw you in. Adventure can make you hungry for more and make you figure out ways to get back to it as soon as you can. Certainly, there are many reasons school can be an adventure—if the circumstances favor it. For that to happen, we had to find ways to change them to favor adventure. Wildlands is framed around learning by doing, being involved, and taking initiative. Every day can be an adventure! But here's what we also learned: adventures need purpose, place, challenge, elements of new experiences, and they need full participation by staff and students alike.

Wildlands Bait Company

When students come in with an idea or project that fits their learning goals, it can really open up a whole new world. One fall, after we had wrapped up our major field season, a senior wanted to create hand-made fishing lures. He knew enough about this process to get started, but he thought it would be a good challenge to turn his hobby into a small business project. As he set about getting the background information he needed, he met with staff and discussed the many possibilities. Before long, he had a plan.

The process for creating the lures had several steps to it. Design, material selection, the craftsmanship components in the shop, the painting, testing, and quality control were all part of the process. There were budgeting, business plans, marketing, and employee management to be considered. Add to this the ever-present cost factors, investment capital for start-up, and accurate record keeping. He had made a few of these lures in his spare time, but now he was recruiting some other students to join his team, develop a production method, form his small start-up company, train his employees, get production going, and set output goals. After scouring the literature and using several great resources about small business development, he built a budget and projected costs, labor, and profits based on price points. He investigated local markets for his lures. As the year went on, his team of "Wildlands Bait Company" produced, packaged, and delivered hand-made fishing lures to a couple local and one chain sporting goods stores. The project was a complete success, but that's not the whole story.

As the bait production project was going on, the young man decided he wanted to learn about the habits of smallmouth bass firsthand. Range, territoriality, and winter behavior under the frozen lake were some of his questions. He worked with our staff and a mentor from a local resource agency to design a project where he could attach radio transmitters to a few fish in a local lake. In order to carry this project out, funding was needed for the transmitters and other supplies. Initiative was the key here. After some research, a few letters, emails, and phone calls, the student obtained funding from some local bass fishing chapters of a national organization. After researching and documenting the background needed to carry out this effort, he and fellow students, well, they went fishing. A couple of trips is all it took to catch some bass. Our staff accompanied them, assisted in the attachment of the transmitters, and helped train the students in the triangulation methods used to obtain accurate location data on tagged animals. He then set about learning the methods for accurately mapping the locations in geographic information systems software.

Consequently, when the national bass group heard about this project, they featured him on their website and print journal and invited him to present his project at their convention. He also set up a booth with his project information and his Wildlands Bait Company lures. Two solid days of talking and explaining the details of his school projects—and selling quite a few lures. In fact, his booth was one of the busiest at the convention! Most of the people were shocked to find out he was working on these things as a high school student. They all asked, "Where do you go to school?" And many sighed, "I wish they had schools like that when I was a student."

Adventures

At Wildlands, we provide students with opportunities and situations where they can try all sorts of new skills and learn through both physical challenge and academic adventure. The sky's the limit for our students when it comes to creating projects they are fully vested and interested in. Students can take risks knowing we will provide them with safety nets, and can learn by being fully connected to adventures where they are key players, problem solvers, performers, and researchers. We have a buddy rule at Wildlands, similar to the military philosophy of "Leave no one behind," and no matter what the adventure, the entire school is behind each student, supporting their mission.

Introducing students to new, atypical, challenging, and stressful situations stretches their personal boundaries. When you push limits and test boundaries, a certain amount of discomfort can occur. We have all probably experienced both physical and intellectual challenges when we weren't sure if we could push through. Sometimes such challenges can even modify the way we see things, or see ourselves. As a staff, we have learned it is necessary to create new adventures, academically and physically, in order to help students break down and push through those barriers. A class of 2013 graduate said it best in a note she left us at graduation: "I've learned to challenge myself beyond what I think I am capable of, and learned so much about teamwork and perseverance. I've learned that being wet is not the worst thing that can happen to you, and with the right attitude a little rain can be a grand adventure."

The most exciting adventure of all is when students become full partners in their learning. They are totally involved. They have to plan, make decisions, find resources, develop methods, defend ideas, and communicate daily to advisors, peers, and even strangers about what they are doing and learning. When learning is connected to the community or issues outside the school, has relevance, and the outcomes are not just to "turn something in," the learning is so much deeper. This is the adventure of learning to be motivated and independent instead of compliant and dependent. When students accomplish this, there is no telling what learning adventure they will go on next.

A "Normal" Day

We can't be out in the field every day, so let's talk about what a "normal" day might look like at Wildlands. On any typical day (well, there isn't really "typical" at this school) as a Wildlands student, you'd arrive at school and check in with your teachers and peers, get your work area ready, and begin to check your project to-do list. Initial thoughts of what you need to accomplish for the day begin swirling around your brain. Which projects are you concentrating on most? What things are pressing and need to be done in shorter time frames? The choice is yours. Perhaps a quick look at your learning plan will help with the decisions regarding what should be tackled first and indicate if there are things you are not yet dealing with. Ideas of how might you design projects to meet some of those goals are quickly written down for reminders later in the day.

Then you meet with a team where you are part of a long-term project, design some new plans, reorganize, and get to work. In the meantime you are also planning some college visits, or perhaps a job shadow. When you need a change of pace, you seize the opportunity talk to a staff member about the formal project proposal you've requested and discuss revisions, timelines, and how to get resources and materials necessary to begin. The day is yours. You need to plan it, know what to do, and do the work of learning and building skills through projects. For many students, this could be an adventure. For most students, it is certainly different.

On another day, you might arrive and meet with all the students in the Morning Meeting and provide the reminder announcement for the field project of the day. Shortly after, you and the entire group get on the bus and head to a local fish farm because the student body is working with the fish farmer to net, capture, weigh, measure, and analyze the fish populations in his rearing ponds. You and your partner responded to the inquiry from the farmer and took the lead to set this project up to meet the needs of the farmer. To start with, you are one of the net operators, then you switch and collect data on all the panfish. At one point, you pull a scale from each fish and label the little bag it goes in with the fish number to match the data collected so you can age each fish to calculate growth rates. When the morning fieldwork is done, the local fish farmer spends some time talking to the group about how he runs the business and all the things he has to consider to raise fish commercially. The group will return two more times before all of the necessary data is collected. You and some of your team will examine those scales, calculate ages, and create reports from the data for the farmer. The best part of this adventure? You, as a student, were in charge.

Mulligan Physics

Students find out much more about themselves when faced with justifying their own learning. Even seemingly simple activities can become adventurous if put in the right light. For example, one afternoon a couple students approached with two or three physics labs they'd finished—or so they thought—and wanted to evaluate them and receive credit. It was clear they just wanted to be done. The labs were part of a series, a very widely used physics inquiry lab learning system. The students had everything done. Or so they said. It is one thing to get the answers and turn them in; it is quite another to be able to explain what you did, why you did it, and what all the numbers actually mean. We told them to take a mulligan, and try it again.

That's when the adventure begins. Where a project-based environment can really create some opportunities for conversations about learning. One of the first rules of PBL is to figure out what you, as a learner, need to know and build your personal knowledge. So until these two could return with explanations about the how and why of the experiments—not just the answer in joules, or calories, or degrees C—the conversation had to continue. It took some encouragement, listening to a little grumbling each time they walked away thinking they were "done," but after a couple days they had it all figured out. At the end, they both realized that they knew the what and the why of their work and could explain it. They had *more* than an answer. They had an understanding.

At a small school with only sixty students (approximately ten per class), nobody can hide. Everyone gets noticed, and they have to work together to learn how a team functions. When they work on a project and learn something, they have to be in charge of closing, helping evaluate, and discussing the outcomes of their own learning. Students can't just say, "Am I done?" or "How did I do?" They have a CONVERSATION! Oftentimes it is more about what they learned by mistake or by thinking how to improve the next time. At the end of each semester, in front of their parents, teachers, and other community members, they have to review their projects and their learning, and discuss their growth and progress.

Owning the Adventure

You might think all this adventure is set up by the teachers for the students to experience. Sometimes that is true, but many times it is not. Most of the new, risky, challenging things are cooperatively generated by students with a staff member's assistance. There are a lot of things that just happen because the students want them to. Once a student lives in this type of learning environment for enough time, they begin to really take the reins and do things that move their learning plan forward. For example, we regularly see students who are involved with our newsletter take over the whole thing. From the planning stages, to the assignment of articles to other students, to the editing, layout, printing, and distribution, the students take care of it. Generally it is one or two students who take the leadership role, and it becomes a very rich and rewarding learning experience as four times during the year they publish an eight to twelve page newsletter. This is where the openness of a project-learning format can really pay off. Open to outcome, and open to student leadership.

Community service projects also pop up all the time, and service learning opportunities arise through student-generated ideas and contacts in the community. The students set them up, recruit team members, inform staff about schedules, transportation, materials and the like, and then go forward and accomplish the goals set. It is amazing to see ninth and tenth grade students come up with ideas, present them to classmates at the Morning Meeting, and get people involved in things like helping the elderly during the winter, serving food to the homeless, raising money for Special Olympics, creating marketing materials for fund-raising events, and volunteering their time and talents to help local organizations. Quite often the students who plan these events get things rolling without teachers helping and regularly check in.

The adventure is always in the journey, the learning, and the doing. We learned very early that adventures were a key to creating context and opportunities that take children to the edge or outside of their comfort zones. Whether it is during the school day or in the backcountry, the adventure is paramount to developing the close-knit, cooperative teams and relationships that allow our school to function as family. Our staff has learned when adventures present themselves, sometimes we have to go for it. Operating in a project world, we sometimes have to step out of our comfort zones and learn along with our students. Being part of the Wildlands family means all of us—students and teachers alike—are constantly being presented with adventures.

You Will Dry

You will dry has become a mantra for our school. It's both a literal reminder that getting wet is not so bad if you are prepared, and a metaphor about taking chances. It's okay to fall in the water once in a while and remember that even when your efforts are "all wet," you will dry. Learn from your experiences, your successes, and failures, and use your adventures as springboards. If school is to be an adventure, we all need to think a bit differently about how we view learning. All learning.

To be sure, a river adventure is one that will stay embedded in the memories of those students as a unique and challenging part of their experience at Wildlands, but it is not only those grand experiences that provide the adventures. It is also the everyday challenges like managing your own time, being able to choose projects, and working with teachers to develop a way to reach your goals. While it may be a reach for some people to call school an adventure, it doesn't have to be. Every day truly *is* an adventure when school is framed around learning by doing, being involved and taking initiative, and when students are full partners in their own learning.

The Flambeau

We were careful to set our canoe up for these rapids just as Paul had suggested. Everything was looking great from the back of the boat, until I realized the front was no longer going down river. Panic began to set in. As the boat spun around, and the waves seemed to grow astronomically in size, I could hear Paul screaming from the rocks, "Just keep paddling!" Wow. What a metaphor for life.

But he was right. If we gave up then, we were literally sunk. The only choice was to keep going, so we did, backwards through the entire rapid section.

I could tell we had made it through when I could no longer hear the sound of the water over the beating of my heart. We were triumphant. And dry. I could breathe again. I looked at my student partner, who was white as a ghost and just started laughing. This was the very first time I had gone through a set of rapids on a river, in a canoe, and not only did we manage to maneuver our vessel through the gushing waters and avoid any major obstacles backwards, but we DID NOT TIP. Victory!

Teaching at Wildlands was my first experience working in the real world, finally doing something I had dreamt of for a long time. In 2005, I was fresh out of college and took a chance to get involved with a brand-new school that I knew would be different. Let's be honest, I needed a job, so I wasn't going to be too picky, but when one of the qualifications for this job was getting a CDL license so I could drive a school bus for field trips, I could have said no. I could have taken the easy way out and waited for a job I was more comfortable with, teaching regular classes in a regular school.

But I took a chance. Every one of us at Wildlands that year took a chance to try something different; to step out of our comfort zone and be open to new possibilities and opportunities; to be at a place that was unlike any other in our area and truly be an integral part of Wildlands; to work together to build a program and a culture from the ground up that would captivate students' interests and help them develop a skill set overlooked by other schools. While I was part of the teacher team providing these students with a different learning opportunity and environment, I know now that these students were helping to open *my* eyes to what's really important in education. Them.

A lot of educators, teacher trainers, and schools will tell you the individual student is what matters. However, the training for teachers focuses on teaching groups, managing whole classrooms, and mass marketing of the learning. The classes I took in college focused on lesson plans, standards, and getting kids to be quiet in their seats. Looking at each one of the kids on this trip, I knew I had learned more in one year at Wildlands about how to relate to a student than I did in four and a half years in college. At Wildlands, we worked to make sure the individual student was what mattered most. Just like on this trip, each person has a role, a skill level, and needs individual attention to arrive at the next destination safely.

A river can be seen as a metaphor for freedom because it flows day in and day out. Certainly the Flambeau had been tamed since pre-settler times, but this section in the state forest was still free flowing. The fact that students "did the paddling" both on this trip and in the newly created culture of our school was cause to celebrate daily. These students had stepped into this new school and taken on a new freedom as well, assuming a new responsibility for their own learning. Much like the river, the students just kept going, navigating, and learning in a new and different way. Each of the victories, big and small, was cause for celebration because they belonged to the students. They owned them. Even though, on both the river and back at school, we all sometimes hit situations where we got "wet," no one ever gave up, staff and students alike.

It wasn't about stopping short on something because you weren't sure you could do it. It was about digging deep, believing in yourself, not worrying about the outcome, and just going for it. We had built a learning environment at Wildlands that was so respectful and caring that it allowed students and staff to let their guard down without the fear of repercussions they might have experienced in previous years. Everyone was able to develop the confidence to try anything, knowing that the group around them would catch them if something happened.

Luckily, that "catch you if you fall" mentality totally carried over to this trip. As the group was making their way through the Beaver Dam rapids, one pair of boys leaned a little too much, took on a few too many gallons of water and, as if it were in slow motion, I watched their boat roll. Some of their gear was tied in, but what wasn't quickly went overboard with them. They were careful to do as they had been taught and took care of themselves first, floating out of the rapids into the slack water below while beginning the task of gathering random gear within reach. Much of their lost gear was already moving downstream and the option to rescue it didn't look good as it spread out all over the river. Not far behind them, I had made it through this set of rapids—facing forward, thank you very much—and was able to see the boys had emptied their canoe of water, rearranged the gear that remained, and were on their way again. A bit wet but smiling nonetheless. Almost as if planned, several boats in front of them on the river had pulled over, and the teams of students formed a line in the shallow part, rescuing all of the remaining gear. Without second-guessing or being instructed, these students were acting out the values Wildlands was founded on, placing teamwork at the top.

I credit this particular group of students with providing one of the best adventure stories I get to tell students for the rest of my life and solidifying the foundation for me on how to be a project-based teacher. Yes, they were students, but they were people first, and the staff at Wildlands made it a point to get to know them as individuals. In order to do this, students need to be given an opportunity to really be themselves. When students are taken out of their comfort zone, you get to know who they are, what they represent, and what makes them unique. With the opportunity to open up a new school with a fresh slate, we had the ability to take students out from behind the desks and let them shine.

The same thing can be said for teachers. Teachers can't be afraid to leave their comfort zone either. It's easy to stick with what you know, but a better example can be set when you learn to be dynamic and flexible, like you expect your students to be. Teachable moments happen all the time, even if *you* are the one learning the lesson. Students need to see the human side of teachers to get a better understanding of what makes each of us unique, too. Finding a way to provide students with an opportunity for a learning adventure together might be the best thing they take away from the classroom, or wherever it is that your adventure takes place. It has forever changed the way I think about teaching and being a teacher.

Reflecting back on this first trip down the Flambeau ten years later, I can't help but think how far I have come as a teacher and how much Wildlands has developed since those early days. Every year we have expanded opportunities for students to challenge themselves both in and out of the school building. To continue the traditions set by those first students we have traveled all over the state of Wisconsin and beyond. Students start every year with challenging trips that focus on teambuilding, personal skill development, and outdoor learning. In the past few years we have expanded our backcountry and outdoor learning opportunities to include trips focusing on ecology, history, government, culture, and geology, and have expanded to more rigorous physical trips like week-long backpacking and lake-to-lake canoe trips. Places like Chicago, Madison, and Washington, DC have also become fixtures in the Wildlands student world.

We have often returned to the Flambeau with different groups of students. I have been fortunate to be on many of these return trips (you could probably call me Sacagawea now). Each time the story is similar, but the cast of characters changes. With each trip I think of that first group of pioneer Wildlands students who helped create the culture of our school. We've been there in good weather and bad, high and low water, cold nights, warm days, and sometimes fought wind and storms. In all cases the students persevered; they hung on; they had little victories and big wins.

The life lessons learned, the skills acquired, and the stories they made will last longer than any classroom discussion or lecture. The opportunities to build and solidify the relationships among students and staff are irreplaceable. The river reminds us of the constant flowing of time, the flow of students through our school year after year, and the opportunity to provide them with anchors to the natural world in places like the Flambeau. Most important the river provides all who journey with us there a unique learning adventure and the opportunity to realize one of the most important lessons at Wildlands: *you will dry.*

chapter 7

Essential #5

Challenge

Increased freedom means increased responsibility.

Imagine you are a student at a traditional school where the day is planned for you from beginning to end. Adults tell you what to do, what not to do, when to change rooms, what to read, when to talk, when not to talk—and you are expected to be compliant and to be controlled.

Then you decide to come to Wildlands.

Now you enter into a project-based learning environment and are a full partner in planning your learning and managing your day. In fact, you're in charge of at least 50 percent of your day and activities. As you advance from one year to the next, you are even *more* of a partner and *more* in charge. You become familiar with the expectations for earning credits, understand standards and learning targets, decide what to work on and when to work on it, and learn to develop projects that have content, skills, and quality outcomes embedded in the plan.

Plus, you have to cooperate with teachers and other students, keep track of your own progress along with your advisors, and you have to meet face-to-face with your teachers to justify the outcomes of your projects. You debrief, demonstrate, and explain what you have done and learned every time you want to earn credit. You have the flexibility and freedom to pursue areas of interest and passion, but you also have the responsibility to keep good records, write about results, meet with advisors, and justify your learning.

You are also an important part of getting things done at school. Perhaps you help serve or clean up lunch, clean the classroom at the end of the day, help take care of computers and technology, or are in charge of the workshop area. Maybe you are the newsletter editor, mentor younger students, or manage the photos and videos taken for the school. The list goes on, but it boils down to this: you have exited the world of being controlled and compliant and entered the world of independence, responsibility, and challenge. Trust is extended to you—and trust is earned—and you are becoming a fully functioning member of our community and school operation. Not the typical set of expectations found in most schools, yet all part of our school's learning community.

The Dramatic Switch

Besides the need to justify your learning and work as a team, becoming a leader and helping others learn is a major part of the challenge in a project-based learning environment. This idea is illustrated by a Wildlands' alumnus who came to us completely disinterested in school. This young man was supposed to be an eleventh grade student, but was credit deficient because he'd missed so much school due to "boredom." His mom enrolled him at Wildlands in hopes that a more independent and personal learning environment might engage his interests. It didn't take long for us to realize that he was extremely talented and very intelligent. In a relatively short period of time, he acclimated to a project world, began exploring things in an in-depth manner, and became a school leader. He even single-handedly managed a small-mammal population survey project where his interest in DNA analysis and research was ignited and allowed to flourish.

So what happened? How can a student who felt disengaged and uninterested in school make such a dramatic switch? We think some of the answers lie in the idea of challenging students in more than the narrowly defined content areas. Students are typically challenged in only a few areas of life at a traditional school: content knowledge, verbal and analytical (math) skills, and maybe the peripheral areas of social interactions or fitting in. They are only assessed in traditional content as well. What about all those challenges that higher education and life throw at our students after high school?

For too long, educational systems have been created to track, rescue, and remediate. Too often this enables students to slip through the cracks and miss out on developing independent and responsible behaviors needed for success outside of school. We firmly believe in a "Do it" mentality and challenge our students daily to take control of their own destiny. We know they are still adolescents and young adults, but by changing the expectations and their roles, extending trust, and helping them assume responsibility for more than just assignments, we have created a school where challenge is accepted and responsibility is built.

Students make choices and are held responsible for their own learning and progress. They are part of the team that designs their education. They can choose the areas, form the questions, and create the opportunities for learning in personally meaningful ways. If they don't, well, this type of learning is probably not the best for them. In fully implemented project-based learning, students are full partners in their school experience and understand the stakes involved in higher levels of responsibility.

Hey! The Neighbors Want a Movie

Envision a scene where a few students are in conversation with a teacher, and an employee of the Beaver Creek Reserve nature center enters the building and approaches the group. He quickly explains that he and the staff of the reserve are writing a grant and entering a competition to seek support for more renewable energy systems. As part of the grant application, they need a highly polished video presentation detailing many of the requirements of the application. He asks if any of our students would be interested in producing a video explaining the renewable energy systems found on the reserve property and introducing a plan to integrate more solar or wind energy on the site.

At this point, eyes are wandering around the group, and teachers and students alike are looking at each other wondering if anyone is interested in such a project. Then one of the boys who had been listening to the request spoke up and said he would like to get involved. "It sounded cool," he said, and he had always wanted to know more about solar and wind power. Not long after he was able to recruit a partner.

There were several meetings with the Beaver Creek staff, opportunities to read the grant application, and in the end they developed a plan, a script, shot sequences, a timeline, and an outline of the video. During the production phase the video team regularly updated their partners at the nature reserve, held screenings and meetings, and worked to constantly improve the product so it met the needs of the grant. After what seemed like a fairly short time, a few weeks at best, the project was due, the grant had to be sent in, and the video had to accompany it. Following the delivery of the final product to the reserve staff, the students had a meeting with their advisor and closed the project for school credit. A few weeks later the reserve received notice their application and video had made the final cut and were one of three grants in the state left in the running. The decision would be made by the people in attendance at the renewable energy fair sponsored by the granting agency. The movie would be shown to the crowd and accompanied by a summary of the grant proposal. People would get to vote.

These boys *had* to deliver. They had to learn about renewable energy systems and they had to become storytellers, movie producers, and team players in a real context. They had to interact with "clients," revise, communicate, and finish on time. These weren't things they had a great background in already. They didn't have step-by-step directions or a page reference they could look up in a textbook. They had to be creative, think for themselves, understand the entire process, and know the content well enough to explain it to an audience of thousands. Their project mattered and it was a big responsibility, but they met the challenge head on.

Unlearning

In order to break or "unlearn" the habits many students have when they arrive at our school, something needs to happen to ease children off their dependence on adults and into independence and autonomy. It's a big shock to students to be thrown into the captain's chair, especially when that chair involves critical thinking, analysis, questioning, designing projects, understanding learning goals, and conversational assessments. It is like handing over the control of a fast-food corporation to folks who have just been eating there. Sure, they've consumed the food but have no idea how it gets created or how to run the business. It is an understanding of process and production versus just participating in the consumption.

It takes a while for students to become familiar with the essentials of project learning. In order to help, we have designed phases for adaptation to project learning. We have found that this phased strategy works well for both the seasoned, senior students and the brand-new ninth graders.

The Five Phases

Phase One: The teacher leads large-group projects.

Phase Two: Students band together and select a teacher advisor, but the students are now more in control of the project; the teacher is there to steer the ship if it gets off course.

Phase Three: Smaller groups of students are completely in charge of their project, and they choose an advisor to help.

Phase Four: Students complete a short individual project on their own.

Then we break from the first four phases and introduce benchmarks and standards for high quality projects to be used for the rest of their career at Wildlands. This is **Phase Five,** sometimes referred to as "Platinum" project characteristics.

Each phase has specific roles defined for the students and staff, and they change by phase. Each phase has a different set of project-learning primary goals that move from general and group oriented to specific and individually focused. The five phases also have their own sets of expectations and outcomes embedded into the process so students know what they are shooting for as they work through the projects. Each phase builds upon the next in terms of project learning and "unlearning" strategies. Keep in mind we are talking about skills, abilities, teamwork, independence, management, and other factors expected in a project-learning school. The content and subject focus of the projects are always highly variable and related to the learning goals of the students involved.

In Book Two of this series we will provide detailed explanations of the five phases, including teacher and student roles, responsibilities, goals, and outcomes. We will also describe how to run each phase to maximize the unlearning potential.

Healthy Ones

One of the very first Phase One projects asked a group of students, "What can we do to be healthier?" The students gathered for a discussion and brainstorming session armed with a big piece of paper, markers, and lots of ideas on what it meant to each of them to be healthy. They began by writing down words, phrases, and ideas: food, organic, exercise, water, no MSG, calories, yoga, beauty, and so on. After a few minutes, and a lot of laughs, the students realized that there seemed to be three different themes staring them in the face. They began to organize everything that was written into the categories of diet, exercise, and mental health. Little did they know at the time, they were shaping this project *perfectly*.

Realizing that one way to be healthy is to be active, the group decided that this was going to be a very active project. They didn't want to sit in the building looking up health sites, recipes, exercise programs, and diets on their computers every day; they wanted to try new foods and activities and learn from experts outside of Wildlands. The group also decided this was going to be a "learn by participation" project. They made a pact that everyone in the group would try everything they were researching. It wasn't necessary to be good at it, or like it, but trying was important. The support and cohesiveness of this group set an example for all of the groups working through the first project phase. Every day they participated in something active, read an article or watched a documentary, kept track of what they were eating in a food journal, and tried to replace one of their "bad" habits with something healthier.

There were also field trips galore, all arranged by different members of the group. This gang traveled to Mayo Clinic to hear a neurologist talk about the importance of sleep at their age, to the farmer's market to meet with an organic farmer and his family and learn about their farm, and to the Just Local Foods grocery store to learn the importance of buying local and knowing where food comes from. They invited a pediatrician to speak on the importance of establishing good nutritional habits at a young age to carry throughout their lives. Activities like ice-skating, tennis, badminton, working out with a personal trainer, and practicing yoga with an instructor were new to most of the group,

but everyone gave it a shot. Several students took turns spending time in the kitchen preparing foods they had found at local markets using recipes that fit in the "real" and healthy food category. A small group focused on things like how to reduce stress and relax, learned about the value of mental health, and then brought the ideas back to the group. These kids were learning so much by following their own curiosity and contacting experts. They began to truly understand how powerful it is to reach out beyond the walls of the school. The learning opportunities grew every time they met someone new. When they made new connections and got more suggestions and ideas from their contacts, it only served to push them to places they would never have gone by themselves.

This group was so excited about what they were learning they had to share it with the rest of the school. The learning and activities were contagious; students from other project teams kept sliding over to see what the healthy living people were doing. The daily doses of watermelon salsa, green smoothies, homemade juice, and bugging everyone about dropping soda in favor of water were becoming effective. The group was creating a new way of looking at health and living, day to day, at school. They hosted a photo contest to get everyone into a friendly activity that promoted moving around, getting outside, finding great photo ops, and being artistic with cameras and cell phones.

When a few students learned about genetically modified organisms (GMO) in the food supply, they suggested we all research this issue and come up with a personal position. One day they held a family focused fun-run for all the students, their families, and anyone else who wanted to participate. The list goes on, but the point is clear: the challenge of creating a project out of a simple question "What can we do to be healthier?" was met—and exceeded—by a team of very engaged students. They set clear goals, they set their path, the work they did was of the highest quality, and they shared with the whole school community (including parents) on our showcase night.

Leave the Pigeonholes to the Pigeons

Setting goals and working toward them is really the essence of PBL. Choice and self-direction are two key factors in creating the ultimate challenge in the project world. The biggest difference between true independent PBL and "just doing projects" in a classroom environment is the goal setting and the personal ownership part of independent projects. The healthy living project illustrates the power of cooperative project learning and demonstrates a process for getting students involved and growing into a world where passion, interest, choice, and their newfound skills direct their learning.

You might notice that throughout this chapter, specifics about content (math, science, English, history, etc.) have barely been mentioned. Honestly, the formats, phases, goals, and checklists we use are adaptable to all the traditional content areas, keeping in mind that most projects are not just one-subject oriented. Most projects are multidisciplinary and have elements, goals, content standards, and outcomes from several of the traditional core areas of academic study. The healthy living project alone boasted learning objectives in the areas of science, health, English, math, physical education, and technology. Project learning eliminates the stark divisions among subjects.

The pigeonhole phenomenon of learning has no place in a multidisciplinary project world. Because students and teachers are managing projects with many learning outcomes, it can become a little tricky to keep track of all the details. Our students all have learning plans that align with requirements from both the state and our local district. Satisfying and demonstrating success via project learning is indeed a journey of "unlearning." Another apparent challenge, especially for the student, is becoming a full partner in the creating, implementing, and tracking of the learning plan. Luckily, we have been using a very flexible web-based project management tool (Project Foundry, as we have mentioned), and it provides a very streamlined, accurate, and convenient way to record progress, track learning outcomes, collect evidence of concepts learned, and embed authentic assessment.

The project-learning phase process addresses many of the challenges associated with moving from one type of educational system to another. Students are challenged, teachers are challenged, and to a certain extent so are the parents. Because learning takes place in a variety of contexts and modes and varies from group to solo efforts, it can take some time getting used to. Parents are often challenged by the nature of the PBL school and want to understand how their child is learning differently. Whether it is the adventurous physical challenges found in pushing limits in the backcountry, or the "all new" academic challenges found in adapting to project learning and "unlearning" old habits, we have worked to create an atmosphere where students are called upon to be full participants and not simply passive learners.

chapter 8

Essential #6

Confidence

**Help students develop a
learning path that they OWN.**

So how does a school embrace **Confidence** as an essential? At Wildlands, we do it by involving students in projects connected to community with results that matter. We help students develop projects that *they* own far more than their teachers. Our students have to deliver—and at a high level—because others are depending on them.

The key to confidence is challenge, as we discussed in Chapter 7, but we also believe strongly in helping students identify their *strengths* and involving them in activities where those abilities can be used for growth, leadership, and confidence—instead of focusing on what students can't do. In traditional schooling, too often the emphasis is on the failed test, the poor skill, an incomplete assignment. Students are put into groups: slow readers, low math skills, poor spellers. Very soon education becomes the pursuit of what you can't do. Of course, all students must work to improve areas of challenge and move forward, but far too many *learn to avoid the things they most need to improve upon* because of all the negative feedback.

Creating situations and experiences where students' abilities and strengths can be celebrated and honored provides them with a new perspective. It's much easier to work on the weak areas when a student feels valued and knows he or she has something GOOD to offer the school community. Switching a student's perspective from, "I'm not good in math and I hate it" to "I'm the one they rely on to create cool graphics for the brochures and posters" provides students with a sense of belonging and opens the door to conversations and a potentially new perspective about that "math stuff"—or any other area where they may lack confidence. It's all about attitude. Students tend to become open to improvement if they have a positive relationship with those around them.

Finally, we also push students beyond their pre-existing boundaries. Be it writing, math, science, a high-ropes course, or a river trip, boundaries need to be identified and crossed. Trying something new, doing it over and over, practicing it, and demonstrating your new knowledge or skill are keys to creating confidence.

May I Have An Assessment, Please?

In my experience at Wildlands, it is not often that teachers encounter students passively waiting for somebody to "give" them knowledge. Instead, students come to *us* looking for resources, ideas, places to visit, funding for projects, guidance, and advice. They even ask for assessments.

The first time this happened, I really didn't make the connection as to how drastically things had changed. A student approached me and asked, "Can I have an assessment, please?" Because I could log into the online math system and schedule an assessment for her, I did. She thanked me and got to work, and I went about my business of the day. On another occasion a student asked me for an assessment to be scheduled after lunch because he needed to complete several more topics; then he wanted to see how he was doing. Then it hit me. My students were *asking* for assessments!

For twenty years in the traditional classroom, words like *assessment, quiz, test,* and *lab test* instilled fear and loathing into all but the very well-prepared students. A chorus of groans would be heard on "pop quiz" days. I recall students pleading for "test extensions" or extra-credit opportunities so they could shore up grades from poor test performances. Now my students are asking: "May I have an assessment, please?"

Wow, what happened? Ownership and confidence. Even though not all students are thrilled to be doing math, taking assessments, and sometimes even going backwards in progress if they forget certain aspects of the subject, they all still ask for that assessment. It could be because they want to know how they are doing. Let me repeat that: the students *want* to know. They are doing the work, they are learning the new skills and abilities, and now they are working with the teacher to schedule progress checks and assessments. These students have a stake in the process and are part of the planning, the doing, the correction of mistakes, and the celebration of accomplishments. It is an amazing shift in paradigm when the thought is no longer about studying or cramming for an exam, but preparing for an assessment so they can check their own understanding and progress. And they are doing it at their own pace at times when they choose to work on it. Does it work perfectly for all students? No. Can it be modified to fit the needs of the students? Yes.

Finding the Situation

The crucial part of building confidence is not returning a rubric with a letter grade on it but, instead, presenting students with a list of observations through a conversation. Yes, a conversation. When students realize that teachers are invested in helping them develop abilities and reach potential and want to help them grow as learners, their level of investment in their own learning skyrockets. It's okay to discuss areas they need to improve on, but having them hear—not read—a few of the items you noticed they did well immediately builds confidence and one conversation builds into the next. This also opens a door to set goals together regarding any areas for improvement and a direct focus for them to work toward.

The majority of students who transfer to Wildlands in the middle of their school years (regardless of grade level) are terrified of public speaking or being on display in front of a group of people. They try their best to remain a member of the crowd for as long as possible (which fared well for them in traditional school), but it is inevitable that within the first few weeks at Wildlands, they are challenged to present something to the group. It might be a formal speech, part of a group presentation, or ideas they might have within a group conversation. They always accept the challenge, though some more reluctantly than others, and make their way through it.

It is incredible to watch a student standing on the graduation stage, delivering a speech that is better written than most professional motivational speakers, and reflect back on how far they have come. Or watch a student team present information they have collected and analyzed regarding a body of water to a town board whose members are picking their jaws off the table in amazement. Maybe the best is watching students present their semester final, a thirty-minute presentation highlighting their projects and accomplishments for the semester using their ePortfolio website filled with hundreds of artifacts. This is done in front of the staff and their parents, who watch them command the flow of the presentation and the feeling in the room. Confidence just radiates out of our students in the way they carry themselves, the deep connection they make with the audience, and the admiration they feel from fellow classmates and staff. They know, without a doubt, they have the confidence to conquer whatever is next.

Mapping the Way

The Beaver Creek Reserve (BCR) had a need for an accurate set of campus maps and the "new and improved" mapping project was pitched to the Wildlands students by the BCR staff. A staff member from the University of Wisconsin–Eau Claire (UWEC) Geography department was interested in teaming up on the project and enlisted a senior geography student to be the lead mentor. During several meetings with the UWEC folks, the BCR staff, and our students, all the stakeholders had a chance to help define the mapping needs.

Wildlands students had to significantly upgrade their knowledge and skills in both the Geographic Information Systems (GIS) and Global Positioning Systems (GPS) fields to deliver high quality accurate maps. The university supplied the cutting-edge GPS units. The UWEC student began arranging tutorial sessions with our team leaders, and they dug into the necessary materials to become experts. In return, team leaders would teach the rest of the field data collectors how to map using the high-tech GPS equipment. Within a very short time the confidence and skills needed to move the project forward had been developed.

The cooperative team of university and high school students had defined all the structure and organization of the mapping effort, the fieldwork, data needs, and computing requirements. Our two team leaders set up schedules, defined data needs, and coordinated the collection of the map data over several months. They had incredible patience and tenacity to follow through with hours of tedious work, troubleshooting, and keeping the group organized.

This project continued for the entire year. From the early meetings, the many, many drafts of the maps, the stakeholder revision comments and requested changes, to the long hours in the field and at the GIS computer, our students stayed on the mission. Not only were they successful, they were confident the product they were delivering met the needs and wants of their client.

The Beaver Creek Reserve Mapping project created an opportunity for students to be involved in a multilevel, multidisciplinary project with a tremendous community impact. Projects like this one overflow with both a wide variety of content and skill learning, and the opportunity to develop confidence as the outcome is a product needed outside of the school environment and not just an assignment.

Hand Over the Keys

I sensed a small amount of nerves in my high school students as fifty-two tiny second-grade students' faces peered out the frosty bus windows pulling into the driveway. Each youngster climbed down onto the snow covered sidewalk and was welcomed by a tunnel of Wildlanders, who gave them high fives and greeted their buddies from the last visit. This wasn't the first time we'd hosted these miniature learning sponges, but it was the first time my students were running the entire program—start to finish—and I was watching in the background with the rest of the teachers.

That day we had invited the second-graders to learn about different states of matter by visiting multiple hands-on stations that had been created by Wildlands students. Without hesitation, one of my student leaders began instructing the second graders to put their coats aside and find a seat quietly so everyone could get started. A team of high schoolers formally welcomed everyone, provided a quick orientation of how the day would go, and broke the students into groups for the day's activities. To the second-graders, my kids looked like a group of professional cast members at Disney, taking charge, explaining everything with a smile, and keeping things moving. I was confident in their abilities and knew it would be a great day.

Each small group took off with their Wildlands "tour guide" directing them to their very first station. Once there, the Wildlands station leaders began their demonstrations and asked lots of questions to get their young buddies thinking about the "state of matter" they were witnessing at that particular inquiry station. Some were working magic with dry ice, others had "goo" that is both a liquid and a solid. There were ice explorations, an ice cream making station, heating and cooling labs for expansion and contraction, gas pressure play, bubbles that floated on invisible gas in aquariums, and other fun activities motivating the visiting students to start thinking. As all of this was going on, the Wildlands photo team was snapping away like the paparazzi capturing the wonder and excitement bubbling out of each of the second-grade students.

Laughter and smiles were the norm as the stations provided excitement, fun, and challenge all focused on the science topic for the day. The flurry of activity and level of noise seemed distracting, but looking at the engagement of ALL students involved, it was easy to see there were multiple levels of learning and teaching taking place. Just before lunch all of the groups had rotated through all of the learning stations, the large group got back together for a recap of what they just witnessed, and before we knew it, it was time to say good-bye to our junior scientists. The second-graders grabbed their winter gear, loaded the bus through another Wildlands high-five tunnel, and were on their way back to their own classroom, grinning from ear to ear.

After a huge sigh of relief, and a bit of discussion about how exhausting teaching kids was, the Wildlands students spent the next hour or so cleaning up and putting things away. After I personally thanked each one of my students, we met to debrief the day's activities, tell the hilarious stories about what happened or was said at their stations, and thought about ways to improve the next time around. I could tell by the looks on their faces they were proud of what just happened—and glad that it was over. Another buddy day successfully carried out by the Wildlands students. When I say carried out, I mean, researched, planned, organized, supplied, scheduled, set up, and executed by the students. On days like that, our staff simply sits back and watches the students create a meaningful and memorable experience for our elementary school partners. We have developed a relationship with our students, and they know that we trust them, and they are self-assured enough for us to ultimately give them the keys and get out of the way.

But How About Peers?

Empowering our students to deliver a day like the second-grade day went to an entirely different level one fall. Over the summer we had made a great connection with the teachers from Northern Lakes Regional Academy (NLRA) in Rice Lake, Wisconsin. They were incredibly curious about our school. They wanted to know how we operate overall, about our teacher-powered and student-centered culture, about our projects, and the power of student leadership. We decided the best way to really explain our school was to have our students show their staff and students how we operate. Students were in charge of the day, 100 percent, from start to finish.

When our students found out they would be hosting high school students, they were initially hesitant. It is one thing to plan activities to keep seven-year-olds amazed using dry ice or homemade ice cream, it's quite another to impress teens their own age. Peers and their expectations are sometimes a little frightening. Plus, it was the first week of school, and they had just a short amount of time to prepare. Nevertheless, our students showed exceptional perseverance, determination, creativity, and confidence in their ability to work as a team. (Even when we lost all computing access during the planning period!)

Amazingly, the schedule worked, dilemmas were fixed on the fly, and the strategies to get NLRA students active and talking succeeded. In just a few hours, students from both schools met, worked together, played together, thought and discussed together, and made some new friends. Perhaps one of the greatest achievements for the day was kicking off a new era where the isolation of the school building and location become irrelevant and collaborative learning became limitless.

Like clockwork, our students took a few minutes after our guests left to discuss and debrief the day. When asked if they would like to try something like this again, they all agreed they would. Even though it had been the first week of school, our returning students had jumped right in and led our rookie students. Together they made it, they delivered it, and they did it with confidence.

We Do Stuff Like This All the Time

During the summers we often work with other teachers to help them develop PBL for their schools. We have held several institutes on our campus where thirty to forty teachers come stay with us for several days to become familiar with how Wildlands PBL works, learn about how our school operates, and be introduced to our school's culture. One summer we designed a PBL immersion course where the teachers were project learners and assumed the role of students to better understand the project process. In true Wildlands fashion we wanted our institute to be unique and different. Because our students are such a significant and integral part of our learning community, we decided to hire five students to help teach and lead the institute. There was no better way for other teachers to see and hear about what happens at Wildlands than straight from the horses'—or students'—mouths. For the duration of the institute our students assumed a central role, working side by side with the teachers, leading discussions, giving presentations, and serving as team leaders on the teachers' mini-projects.

The teachers who attended were from all over the state. A couple had several years in the PBL teaching environment, but generally, most had fewer than four years, and many were brand-new or in the first year or two of a PBL school. After spending three days exploring student-centered learning, the teachers were asked to present their plans or "take away" projects they had prepared to use in their own schools. A variety of projects and plans were presented on that last morning, and one in particular caught our attention, not so much for the nature of the project, but how it was developed.

There was a young teacher who had only been working in the PBL format for one year. She came to our institute excited to experience all the possibilities our staff and students would share, and took the opportunity to participate in many of the group projects. When it came time for her presentation, it was evident these three days had built her confidence and enthusiasm as a PBL teacher. As she stood in front of thirty colleagues for her final presentation, she talked about how thrilled she was about the water quality and stream investigation project she had completed with her partner. Their school had purchased a bunch of resources for water quality testing with grant money but hadn't utilized them up to this point. After three days at Wildlands, all of the materials, test kits, and methods made sense, and she couldn't wait to use them with her students—thanks to a Wildlands student who'd jumped right in to help her saying, "We do stuff like that all the time. I know what to do. Let me help you."

This student single-handedly pulled out all the materials, equipment, procedures, and background resources and began to share them. She helped get the project started, demonstrated the background required, ran through the fieldwork and water tests, helped with what the results meant, and then helped design some simple activities to get the teacher's students' feet wet in this area of study. All of this was mostly impromptu—and in fewer than two days!

Our student didn't need to ask for permission; she understood what it meant to be an independent learner, and in this case a full-blown teacher! She knew how much our school values initiative and solution finders. She knew where everything was, how it worked, how to implement the processes, and she took off and helped without thinking twice. Wow, what true project-based learning (and teaching), and what a demonstration of confidence to just jump in and go!

Confidence is embodied in the ability to act, to do, and to know you are moving in the right direction without having to look around for permission, or check in all the time to see if you are right. This student had the confidence to become the teacher *herself*. This story is a prime example of how our students come to understand how the world of learning works at Wildlands. Our students know they don't have to be told what to do or ask permission to learn. They just need to ask for the resources and materials they need to move forward.

Taking on Challenge without Hesitation

Moving from a passive receiver of information in a traditional classroom to a partner in planning and carrying out one's own school experience can be a difficult journey for many students. It also requires a giant leap for the teacher. From the teacher's perspective, one can no longer be wedded to the idea that we are the only font of knowledge. The idea that the curriculum is limited to what the teacher knows is no longer true as students can access resources at the touch of a finger on their laptop, tablet, or phone. As teachers, we are the adults in the room, and we do have the ultimate responsibility for the students making progress in learning, but we have to admit we just don't know it all—and never will. In our school, it is absolutely necessary to develop a partnership with the student and parents, have conversations about goals, strengths, weaknesses, and dreams, and also work to develop a relationship where the student feels the teacher is there for "them" instead of just being there for the subject or curriculum. This idea is paramount to moving toward a shared sense of responsibility for learning. To be willing to ask questions right alongside our students, search for solutions, and chart new pathways for learning is a change in the role of a teacher.

Providing students the opportunity to try, fail, try again, fail again, and keep going allows them to develop perseverance and confidence. Instead of the fear and loathing brought forth by the end-point test environment, repeated failure ultimately helps our students become "in charge" of their learning. We like to ask the kids: Would you like to know half of it, be done with it, not remember it down the road, and get an average grade? Or would you like to stick to it until you know what you are doing, can show what you have learned with confidence, and then move on? Which choice do you think most students make? Which choice has ownership?

In the final analysis, we feel learning is an entirely personal activity and one that should never end. If we as a school are to promote learning, we need to promote habits among both students and staff that are geared toward open-ended outcome, unexpected consequences, and a sense of personal involvement. Many can look up the facts, learn the formulas, or repeat the storyline of a lesson. The real question is: Why do they do it? Is it to learn more, follow curiosity, and answer questions with a true attitude of involvement? Or is it because someone told them to do it? At our school it really does come down to confidence and ownership.

Confidence is the key to taking on life's challenges. In a traditional school, many students are confronted daily with their shortcomings and areas of weakness and become disengaged and unplug from even the best of classroom environments. When the challenge is only that which is set up by teachers in curricular areas, the connection, relevance, and meaning of the challenge is often missed by many students. Students see teachers as the expert and many teachers feel they have to be, but in reality, the students are the ones we want to become experts.

The staff at Wildlands is not afraid to tell our students from the get-go that we don't know everything. We are also not afraid to ask our students for help with a program, or ask how they figured something out. It's a lesson in itself to have students see you, a teacher, as a regular human continuing to learn something new on a daily basis while empowering *them* to teach *you* something. What a confidence builder when they go home at night and can tell their parents how they showed their teacher the best way to accomplish something or educated the teacher about what they just learned.

Putting students in the driver's seat, involving them in real problems, projects, and issues that require performance and delivery are challenges that build confidence, even if they fail. When failure is viewed as learning, perhaps as one way *not* to do something, the students win, and they will take on new things without hesitation. Maybe that is just one definition of this essential idea of Confidence: taking on new experiences and opportunities without hesitation.

chapter 9

Essential #7

Place

**School is not just a building.
It is a place students have
deep connections and want to be.**

We see **Place** as a state of mind, a way to see yourself and how you fit into your environment. At Wildlands, we believe that school should be a place where students want to be, where they need to be—and love to be. To establish this place means encouraging students to be part of something bigger than themselves, to belong, to fit. It means creating a space that nurtures and inspires their passion to learn, to explore, and to achieve their goals. Here's what we know: when students feel that the school is theirs, they shape it and represent it. They feel deeply connected to and take real pride in learning, working, and progressing. At Wildlands this "Place" can be in our building, on an expedition, volunteering, or anywhere you find a Wildlands student engaged.

It's actually not uncommon for Wildlands parents to tell us that their children want to get back to school to work on projects and even want to go back to school from holidays and long vacations! Parents ask, "How do you teachers do that? How do you get students to *want* to be here?" All we can say is that we treat their children like people, like valued members of our community with important roles. Instead of having students learn or work *for* us, we work *with* them on the learning path they choose. We extend to students our trust and provide them with the opportunity to develop personal ownership of their learning. In doing so, we believe they return that trust by their desire to be here and by growing into fully functioning members of our school community.

Owning the Place

Because we are a teacher-powered school, we take on all the responsibilities of running the school. We don't have secretaries or aids. We don't have janitorial staff, bus drivers, or school records people, and most of our computer needs are handled internally with some assistance from our district IT expert. With sixty students and four full-time staff members, everyone needs to pitch in to get the job done, whatever it is. Students included. As a result, we have developed a student service corps, or some may call it job corps. Whatever you want to name it, our students have to play a pivotal role in keeping our school running on a daily basis. Photo specialist, videographer, yearbook editor, lunch coordinators and assistants, computer specialists, community outreach coordinators, equipment managers, website developers, and shop managers are all examples of the roles students can apply for. Resumes are prepared and letters of inquiry are written. We bring in community members to interview and recommend students for the various positions. Students are then briefed on their responsibilities, work with staff to get started, and become even more indispensable members of the Wildlands team. Our students even complete responsibilities like light janitorial clean up of our building. Bottom line? We all take care of our school. It is our place.

You could say that our students own the school. They know how it works, all the *stuff* and *things* there belong to them and it's their responsibility to take care of them, and that builds ownership and pride, but it's more than just ownership of stuff. It's ownership of their surroundings, the freedom to choose daily goals and activities, responsibility for daily chores and school jobs, and an important role in school structure that provides students with a true connection and the strong desire to *be* here.

The Welcome Mat

Over the years, teachers from other districts, parents, interested community groups, school administrators, and many others have visited us. More often than not, they are greeted by a student or two and welcomed in, like being welcomed into someone's home. Typically they are introduced to student tour guides and get the grand tour. In fact, it's not uncommon for visitors to spend most of their time *with students only* and to seek out a staff member only for any last-minute questions before they leave!

Showcase Nights are another way our school establishes a unique feeling of place for our entire Wildlands family. These events are planned, organized, and run entirely by students. It's their night to open the doors to their school and show it all off. The staff members assume a back seat role and advise with the preparations but, when the night rolls around, we sit in the back of the room and smile. Actually, that's an understatement. Saying we grin from ear to ear isn't even strong enough. Watching our students work incredibly hard throughout the duration of the project—which includes preparing for the night's live audience—and eloquently explain the planning, the process, and the variety of outcomes they have learned adds a level of pride to our school that can't be explained. Allowing students to be in the spotlight with their project work adds meaning, makes it matter, and provides them context to do their best. Inviting people in to be a part of it brings everyone closer.

Have to Go or Want to Go?

For the past century, a scene similar to this has played out in cities, suburbs, and small towns: we send children off to the first day with a backpack and a box of supplies so they can reconnect with classmates and friends, meet their new teacher, and start the next leg of their educational journey. In the early grades, many children look forward to a new school year with anticipation, a sense of wonder, and curiosity. Somewhere along the way a good portion of our children begin to lose that, and it's replaced with the *have to do* mentality. What happens to these children who lose touch with the enjoyment of learning? As they go from grade to grade and become less engaged in their own future, what drives them away from curiosity? What takes away initiative? There are probably almost as many answers to those questions as there are children it applies to. One answer could be the lack of place—the lack of ownership of one's surroundings and destiny.

Fit the Students to the Place or Fit the Place to the Students?

The movement in our country toward standardization has created fewer and fewer options for places that fit our students, with more focus on everything *but* the students. When school is a place that focuses only on the systems, content, and institutional culture that have developed in the past century, it becomes less of a place where students *want* to go and more of a place where students *have* to go. The principles of freedom and participatory democracy are evident in the culture of places where people are empowered to make choices and those choices have real outcomes. On the other hand, when choice and voice are absent, the opposite is true. It is all about how the students see *themselves*.

We had a student a few years back who'd been kicked around from school to school for quite a while. Each year, for several years in a row, he had moved to a new school. His attitude toward school, teachers, and honestly, most other students, was very poor to say the least. He really didn't see himself as a student or a learner. His goal in school seemed simple: get out of where he was. As a result, he applied to Wildlands, made it through the lottery, and joined our school one fall. His track record of success in school was nonexistent, he didn't want to do anything, and he just wanted to be away from where he had been in previous years, but Wildlands was an option, and he needed options.

Sadly, this is not a miracle success story. His social network outside of school, family issues, and other factors created a world where school was really not important to him, and he only lasted a little more than a year and moved on again. Even though our school didn't completely fit his needs, one small nugget of success was unearthed from the experience: after a couple months at our school and having the opportunity to begin to assimilate into the culture and day-to-day life, he approached some staff in the school office. He closed the door while tears welled up in his eyes and said he wanted to tell us something. He said that for the first time in many years he felt as if he belonged somewhere, that he was treated like a person. *This was the only place he felt at home*.

This is a sad tale. Children *need* places where they belong, and feel safe, needed, and valued. Granted this young man had a very difficult home life, but think about all the detentions, time in the principal's office and suspensions he had endured in other schools. All we did was asked how we could help him, encouraged him, gave him a role in our community, and nudged his behaviors now and then with important conversations about what it meant to be a member of our family. He was in an environment where all the students had voice and were part of the everyday operation of the school. Place *can* make a difference. It comes down to whether we are trying to fit the students into the place or trying to fit the place to the students.

Where You Belong

Our students know they are valued members of our school community because we want to know what they think about how the school operates. When things go well, they let us know, and when things don't go so well, they also let us know. If you think back to the story of the five phases of project learning (Chapter 7 "Challenge"), it details how we help students develop into independent project learners. Well, there is a little more to the story. After the eight or nine weeks of working through the phases and developing some really great projects and learning outcomes, some of the students approached us and wanted to talk about the whole process. It was obvious this method didn't meet with rave reviews from all the students in the building.

We sensed the uneasiness among some of the students and asked them to join us in a debriefing of the process. The students pointed out some very valuable observations about how to change, improve, and reformat the five phases to best suit our student population. The juniors and seniors were incredibly insightful in realizing the younger and newer students needed the larger group projects, guides, and learning labs to develop project-learning skills. They offered to take the lead on these kinds of projects and help build good quality learning projects for their young peers. They also let us know that they were not really very keen on being simple participants in the early phases. They felt it held them back and put a hold on their goals, and they were chomping at the bit to get going on projects they wanted to do. The simple solution: put the experienced students in charge of the early project development phases. Let them propose ideas, recruit team members, and lead by example. Why didn't we think of that?

We feel strongly that if we didn't have a place, a school culture, where the students see themselves as part of the whole process, they might not have spoken up. They knew we wouldn't take offense to what they were saying. They knew their opinions mattered and their suggestions would be heard, discussed, and used. They knew enough not to be whiners and grumblers in the background, but to be solution finders and move everyone forward. Those meetings resulted in students thanking the staff for listening, understanding, and utilizing their ideas. We couldn't be happier as teachers because we know our students are in a place where they recognize their input matters and the focus is on their needs.

Trust and Ownership

Interestingly enough, when it comes to Wildlands, it is not only the students who want be there; the adults are just as committed to being there as well. Many ask us about how all this works. That's a good question because this is *not* a typical teaching job in a typical school, and every single day is different and a new challenge.

What is the biggest difference between how our staff views our roles and those of a more traditional teaching environment? The simple answer is trust. Trusted by the school board to do the right thing for the district and its students. Trusted by the parents to help their children learn, achieve, and grow. Trusted by school administration to create and operate a school that meets the needs of the children who attend in ways that are not offered elsewhere in our district. Trusted to use

our best judgment to put systems and learning opportunities in place that work for our students. Most importantly, we are trusted by our students to do the right things for them: to push them, provide safety nets, open doors, and challenge them.

Creating a school without someone telling us exactly what to do or how to do it provided the realization that the only option was to take charge and build a place with students at the center, literally starting from the ground up. In addition, it had to be successful, or the doors would close. This was *nothing* like setting up a grade book for six sections of students in the fall and turning in lesson plans each week. We were given real trust, real control, and faced with real consequences. The path was not clear from the get-go; there were many starts, retreats, regroups, forge aheads, and left turns. Over time the path became clearer, even though there was no canned method, no book, no curriculum guides on how to build a PBL school with a science and outdoor focus; we gained confidence by making it up, creating it on the fly, and in many cases, building the plane while it was in the air. Every day was a test of the plane, making sure it stayed in the air, and in our case, making sure the students were successful, both here and when they moved on after Wildlands. We have been in a constant state of self-examination, reflection, and review as a school since year one, and this process is the same year after year. This place needs to deliver—the students need to succeed—or this doesn't work.

Keeping the students, their needs, interests, and strengths as the central focus of the school is and always will be our primary goal. We try to create ways to meet the needs of all the students; thus, things like personal learning plans and individual projects became critical. We had to build the core of the school around accepted state and national student goals, benchmarks, and standards, but *how* students achieved and learned could be very different from the traditional classroom. After ten years of working with students in the project- based world, the variety and depth of experiences and methods to meet student needs have only grown year after year.

We all like working here as teachers because our school looks a lot like real life. It provides the environment and culture to get to know students for more than forty-five minutes a day. Students work with staff to develop their own learning plan. Cooperative planning, conversations, reflection, and revision of plans happen all the time. Students and staff come to the school each day and have responsibilities, goals, projects, and things to work on. It functions more like a business than a scripted school day. No day is ever the same.

Student projects drive the activity of the day setting up meaningful conversations about learning, content, growth, quality, evaluation, and skill development. We can integrate learning into all types of activities and have students carry out projects related to our pursuit of lifelong outdoor recreational skills. Camping, rock climbing, ropes courses, community service, and projects with community organizations all have multiple outcomes for students. Science projects with local resource agencies, marketing projects that are actually used, writing for our website or newsletter all become part of the fabric of the place. These projects put the students in the roles of *worker* and teachers as advisors or managers of the learning path. The school staff has a professional environment of constant improvement, self-reflection, collaboration, responding to student need, and self-determination.

The staff believes that *the buck stops here*. If it doesn't work, we change it. If it works, we try to improve it.

The real bottom line about founding and building a learning culture drastically different from other schools is that everyone looks at us differently as well. We have to be held to a higher level of accountability and deliver results. A challenge of this caliber is not for everyone; luckily, our school had the right team at the right time. The excitement surrounding the creation of a new kind of school was contagious, and everyone involved has worked tirelessly since the beginning to constantly meet the needs of the students and families that choose the school.

The success of the school is deeply connected to the success of the students, the satisfaction of the parents, and the ability of the staff to respond to the needs of the students. We have to provide the environment for a high quality experience and educational journey, or we don't get to stay open. Move it or lose it. All involved (staff, students, parents) have a voice in the school community. It allows us to develop and maintain a learning culture that places very high value on individual responsibility, learning how to learn, planning, time management, teamwork, quality, and the partnership between students and staff.

By starting this school our staff was confronted with the issue of transforming the way we worked with students. Transforming the school day. Transforming the climate and culture of school to be more of a learning community where students drive the learning. We had to ask new questions and involve the students in those questions and the quest for answers and solutions. What do successful people do? What makes a school, business, or organization stand out? Many of the answers we found pointed to several very important factors: people want to be there, they care, and they are committed to continuous improvement and self-reflection. They have ownership and are internally motivated. (If you haven't read it, get Daniel Pink's book *Drive* as it outlines some real critical points about motivation, learning, and ownership.) These factors all contributed to creating a

school where the staff is obviously setting the tone and has to provide student-centered services. In this school, the staff often hands over the keys to the students but has to make sure the car doesn't crash. They can't be in the driver's seat if we are.

The teacher's role is another reason we like working here. We are responsible for the students, all day, every day. We all know them and work side-by-side with them. We all get to stand back and understand how the place operates, what needs to be done to improve. We all help each other move forward in our roles. As teachers we all share responsibilities and roles as necessary, not as assignments; if it needs to be done, we do it. It makes us keep our eyes open for all sorts of jobs, both with students and in the operation of the school, and makes for a dynamic and responsive staff. Connecting with parents adds a dimension to this place that many teachers never get to really experience. We have an open-door policy for parents so they can understand what their child is doing and learning. We talk to parents every day via email, text, by phone, and in person. Parents stop by all the time, before school, sometimes during the day, and after school. We like parents to feel comfortable just coming in to chat about whatever they'd like, no appointment needed.

As a small school we can control our day. We all can drive the school bus, allowing us to go on local trips anytime we need to. There aren't three layers of red tape to go through to get our students into the field or to a museum; we just plan it, get parent permission, and go. Again, it's all about *trust*. When a staff member needs to take care of something out of the building, we all cover for our colleague, we keep the school going without hiring substitute teachers, and we share responsibilities. As has been said before, but not often enough, the buck stops with us. We are never in the same place twice, never teach the same thing the same way twice, and can use a variety of resources, locations, and ideas to get students involved in topics. It's our choice as teachers and their choice as students.

Why do we like working at Wildlands? We get to work with our students, plan with our students, help each of them through a variety of paths they help chart. Bottom line? *We* have ownership too, just at a different level than our students. We care because this place is ours and we really get to make a difference. We don't just like this place. We love it.

Part III

So Now What?

chapter 10

How's It Going?

They said it couldn't be done. In fact, lots of people looked at us like we were crazy. We'd given up our classrooms, left established jobs, ventured out to a new location with students from seven different school districts, and started a school without any equipment or supplies for the first three months. Even many of our former colleagues were naysayers. We heard comments like, "What are you doing out there? Counting acorns?" Sometimes these comments were said in jest, sometimes said more seriously. We heard project-based learning was a fad, too different for our area. We heard how charter schools were only for the "bad" kids or the ones that flunk out and are at risk. We heard that nobody would send their kids to this new kind of school.

Many said it couldn't be done, but we believed it could. We grabbed change, embraced it, and fought for it. Along with fighting stereotypes and misconceptions, we had to create a whole new paradigm by educating parents, recruiting students, and trying to establish a track record of success. We were under the microscope with a higher level accountability than ever before in our careers, and we had to deliver— or close the doors.

Well, the doors are still open. Wider than ever.

Wildlands has demonstrated that change can work. We've had ten years with students and eight years with a waiting list that only seems to grow. Our local administrators and school board members remain very supportive, and we have extremely strong parent satisfaction. Our community support is strong, too. The student-produced newsletter (sent out four times a year) attracts donations to help our school provide even more opportunities for our kids.

Perhaps best of all, 75 percent of our graduates have either graduated from or are currently enrolled in two- or four-year degree programs. Post high school, our students have strong grade point averages and many are on deans' lists. They've successfully completed their degree programs, have strong job performance, and lead successful military careers. Our alumni often tell us how valuable the "different" experience at Wildlands was in preparing them for college and tech school. The bottom line: Wildlands is thriving and we are eager to share with anyone who wants to know more.

Spreading the Word

School groups from across the state visit us every year. Even some from other states and a couple of international groups have stopped in to see how it all works. A group of regional superintendents have held their annual meeting at Wildlands for a real glimpse at the kind of projects our students are working on. We have hosted four teacher trainings during the summers to assist other PBL teachers with building innovative schools, creating a student-centered culture, and managing projects. Other school districts have modeled their project schools after our general concept, and we have helped them get off the ground.

We host teachers for immersion experiences during the year so they can be side-by-side with our students and learn about PBL. We train, coach, and mentor people from other schools and school districts as they develop PBL, teacher-powered schools, and the building of positive student- centered school culture. Our students have even helped us teach other teachers about the project world. Several local agencies and citizens groups have come to us asking to team up on projects, and some have requested data from projects we have done.

A few years back, we joined with some other schools across our state and helped found a grassroots teacher and school development network for innovative school models. The **Innovative Schools Network (www.innovativeschoolsnetwork.com)** now has over 170 partner schools across our state, is growing nationally, offers a wide variety of services for transforming schools, and we participate in many of their conferences and trainings. For many years we have also worked hand in hand with **Project Foundry (www.projectfoundry. org)**, the web-based tool for managing, aligning, and assessing student project-based learning. The partnership with Project Foundry works both ways. Sometimes they contact us for input regarding their ideas and improvements, and other times we suggest new features. Many of the features in their software came about through suggestions from our staff to make the project world easier to manage and operate in. As a student-centered, project-based school, we could not effectively manage the learning process wihout this system.

Measuring Success

There are many ways to measure success. Our staff has many ways to ask "How's it going?" and is engaged in this questioning all the time, not just to see if a student says, "It's going okay," but to *really* get to the heart of the matter. We want to know how the students feel about their work, their learning, their experiences at school, and what they need or want. We do this by examining all kinds of work, including artifacts, demonstrations, written and spoken communication, project results, models, student-led seminars, discussions, ePortfolios, experimental results, project process and flow that all give us a window into the student as a learner.

Every student is scheduled to present at a semester-end review conference. They prepare for a thirty-minute presentation reflecting back on the semester using their ePortfolio where staff and parents listen and discuss their progress, learning, projects, goals, grades, and credits earned. We joke that these conference are "justify your existence" sessions, but it is true that project learners have to be confident in the outcomes and justify their learning objectives. These conferences and presentations get stronger every year. When people ask, "How do your students do?" they are mostly focusing on that narrow set of knowledge reflected in standardized tests. Well, we can answer they score as well if not better than most schools. As a matter of fact most score far above average, and of course, some have difficulty because they are individuals.

Testing at Wildlands

The only standardized tests our students take are the ones required by the state and the school district. The standardized testing environment can be very stressful for some students. We always try to put things into perspective when our students have to travel this road. One year a student wrote a letter of support for a teaching fellowship and had this to say about the tests.

"Just this morning, as we were getting ready for state testing, he said, 'You know, even if you don't score as high as you think you should have, this doesn't diminish who you are as a person.' I was really nervous about the test until he said that. It made me feel confident and helped me not to stress out as much as I would have."
—Tenth grade student

The state tests called Wisconsin Knowledge and Concepts Examination, or WKCE, were given every year, until 2015, at multiple grade levels. Students could score in one of four categories, minimal, basic, proficient, and advanced. Proficient and advanced are the score levels considered "passing" when people use the test to see if schools measure up. The percentage of students in the proficient and advanced categories has become the measuring stick. There is a state average, and then there are scores for schools. (We still participate in the state assessments but they seem to be changing almost seasonally due to political whims.)

At Wildlands, students in seventh, eighth, and tenth grade took the WKCE in the fall. Here is a sampling of the results from a few recent years. We have grouped all the students and represent our results as a whole school. These results can also be seen on our website on the "About Us" page at **www.wildlandschool.net/about_us.phtml**. The percentages shown are the students who scored in the "advanced or proficient" categories, (the top two) on all the tests. Again, this is an average of all our students on all subject area tests: math, science, reading, language arts, and social studies.

% of Students Scoring Advanced or Proficient

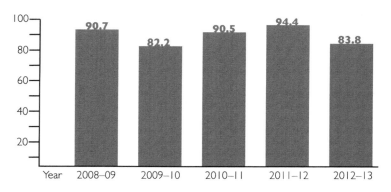

When examining these numbers, we always have to remember how percentages and statistics can be used in more than one way. On one hand, this shows that of all the students who took the state standardized assessment in our school in 2010–11, 90.5 percent of all their results in all categories were in the advanced and proficient categories. On the other hand, it doesn't show that in some testing groups—for instance, the tenth grade—there may have only been five students tested, meaning each student can sway the results of that grade by 20 percent. When the numbers are small, the statistics become less meaningful. For people who want to see these kinds of test results, we can provide them, but we can't say it enough that the high stakes standardized test is really not the measure of any student's true abilities.

It is too bad that we can't report on how our students interact with the people at the Community Table when they volunteer to cook and serve food for the homeless, or how they present to civic and government groups about the results of their projects, or how they plan, budget, and build trail improvements on the nature reserve where we are located. There are no standardized tests for how they help the second and third grade students during our buddy program or plan and prepare for backcountry trips.

It is hard to score and report on the way the students lead tours for adults that visit our school, manage their own science labs, conduct student-led book groups, help each other peer edit and produce our newsletter, or help manage our lunch program and maintain our computers. The state doesn't have a way to measure the performance assessments we use for projects or report on how independent students become when they are highly functioning project learners.

We Love Feedback!

Asking students and parents what they think of their experiences at our school is a critical component for school improvement. Meetings with individual students and small groups of students take place regularly to debrief, discuss, and suggest improvements in our school. It used to be difficult to get students to be really open and honest in these kinds of meetings, but as we have developed the supporting culture which values everyone's input, students now regularly step right up and offer their ideas. We also have held strategic-planning meetings with our students to set annual school improvement goals and work to help the students set personal goals that align with the school priorities. Everyone has a voice and a chance to help shape the direction of improvement.

Talking to parents is also a must, and we also have sent out parent surveys to gauge the school's performance and to get suggestions and feedback. Here is what parents have had to say on some of our surveys over the years.

> "As a former member of the Eau Claire school board, I am truly impressed with the amount of community service and involvement your school focuses on. It is by far the most I've ever seen."

> "This year, my son is a freshman. During midsummer last year, he started having second thoughts about possibly wanting to go back to the regular school system because of the high school environment and missing out on the whole high school experience. He opted to stay at Wildlands and is very happy that he did. I've asked him a few times if he'd rather go to a normal high school when various activities have been going on in my daughter's school. He consistently responds that he has no desire to leave Wildlands—ever! (Until he graduates that is!)"

> "The project-based learning is how I think all schools should be run. The girls can take credit for the learning that happens. They can conceive an idea and be encouraged to carry out a project based on their idea. There seems to be just the right amount of guidance to keep my girls focused but enough freedom to allow the disequilibrium to transform into real learning."

"My son has attended Wildlands School for three years now, starting in seventh grade. This is the best academic environment a parent could hope for their child! The hands-on learning, the equipment and tools available to him, as well as all of the different types of projects have been of such benefit to him. He is always enthusiastic about going to school, and his grades reflect this. (He never wants to stay home—even when he's not feeling well!) His excitement when he discusses his projects with us is something we don't see from his sister who is in a regular public school. He has a clear understanding of everything he is working on. We are always impressed when we see his results on the standardized testing used to judge his academic progress. We were never able to say these things when he was in regular public school. Although always a good student, he did not have the self-motivation to learn as he does now."

"Our son has been attending Wildlands for three years. He started in seventh grade and currently is in ninth grade at Wildlands. The school has been a wonderful learning opportunity for our son. The hands-on outdoor learning environment fits his learning style. He has grown in so many different areas, including leadership skills, assertiveness, confidence, interest in exploring careers, and interest in the environment around him. The staff is caring and strives to provide the best learning opportunities for each student. Wildlands is a small, friendly school, and seems like a family. I enjoy volunteering at the school because I believe that it provides a unique learning opportunity for students. It is a great way to support the school and to augment our son's educational experience. We would highly recommend Wildlands School as a wonderful educational experience for middle and high school students."

We also utilize a school improvement and staff development model that we created, enabling a constant focus on moving both the school and the staff forward. By meeting regularly throughout the year to set school, student performance, fiscal, and community goals, we have a process for staying on target as we move the school forward each year. Periodic reviews of goals and progress help us keep on track and adjust to meet changing needs.

Teachers also set individual professional growth and development goals that we integrate into the annual school improvement effort. Our teacher-powered staff conducts a 360-degree peer evaluation process based on both the involvement of staff in school goals and each of their personal plans. This process has yielded consistent forward motion, innovative development, and the ability to be flexible and respond to student and school needs.

In the traditional teacher evaluation model, a supervisor is trained to evaluate staff. Our staff works *cooperatively* to help one another develop as professionals. The systems in place for high-stakes teacher evaluation don't have the foresight to make teachers accountable for each other and their schools. Top-down manufacturing models encourage compliance and discourage innovation and independence. We feel our teacher-powered school improvement and evaluation model provides a pathway to *consistent* self-evaluation and quality improvements instead of one-shot evaluations and grading.

The Family Tree

Once you are part of the Wildlands family as a student, parent, sibling, volunteer, or partner in a project, you are forever a part of the Wildlands family. It's just like when kids grow up and move out of the house. They aren't there anymore, but they'll always be your kids and you cherish the moments they come back to spend time with you. (And since we don't have any money they can ask for, we know they genuinely want to visit with us!) We often have alumni and former students' parents come back to visit, send us emails, or post comments that remind them of Wildlands on social media sites. They are just as curious about what is going on at Wildlands as we are about how far they have soared to this point in their lives.

During the week before Christmas, our school has a slew of visitors. The first to show up are almost always the college freshman who can't wait to tell us all about the first semester. Most come smiling with a twinkle in their eye and a list of stories about papers, classes, new friends, dorm life, and how they are having a grand time. We always do the standard Wildlands interrogation and pry into how prepared they felt hitting this new institution and if they struggled, excelled, or just cruised along.

As we have mentioned, being a project-based school means there are no regular "tests," they don't have to take "lecture notes," and many students leave somewhat concerned about those skills at the college level. But what we find out is many times they feel that *they are more prepared than most of their classmates* because they have a background in projects and managing their own time. Wildlands alumni also tell us how they know how to manage the non-class time and be productive because they have always had to set up their own day. In college they only have a couple "big" assignments or projects that add up to the grade in a class.

Most high school students come from "daily" work, worksheets, and regular quizzes, and are very regimented in courses. Wildlands graduates know some of the most important skills are to be able to seek quality information, work with advisors and staff, and synthesize ideas from a variety of sources. They report regularly that contacting and using college professors is no big deal because they are used to asking and clarifying their roles and responsibilities. Professors don't always include everything in lectures, and many students speak about back checking and referencing what goes on in classes using a variety of resources. These are skills they developed as project learners. Sometimes, we even have alumni asking us for advice or reporting back with something like the note below:

Seubert,

I've been finding some very interesting studies on job readiness. There was a study conducted by an engineering company in Australia. They were looking for U.S. graduates to start right out of college. They found that about 80 percent (don't have it in front of me but it was around that percent) of US graduates were not prepared to start in their career. The graduates knew the material but could not apply it in real-world applications because they simply didn't know how. On a test, or pen and paper they could figure things out if the question was asked in certain form but could not do it on their own. That's where I've been finding that the US is missing the difference between performing well on tests vs performing well in life (home, work, or in public).

By the end of this paper I feel like I'm going to understand more about it than some of the people controlling it! (*cough* Legislators *cough*) Maybe one day I'll change that: Run for Senate 2028…

Have I ever told you guys you're awesome? And that you're the best school ever?

Parents often send a note or even stop by to tell us how their college student is flourishing, participating in community groups and service, and unafraid of trying the new things college unveils for them. Parents are happy to credit the project-learning environment and Wildlands as a springboard to the independence and discipline required to survive in post-high-school worlds. Here's what one student's mom sent to us during his freshman year:

Hi Wildlands!

Did you hear my son is a published app developer for Apple?? He has a couple more that he's working on as well. Overall, college is going well for him. We were pleased with his first semester grades. We were concerned at first coming from the Wildlands environment going into the college classroom environment. However, we found out that Wildlands was probably the best prep he could have gotten for college. He received many compliments from his professors at how thorough his research and reports are!

Thanks for all you, Wildlands, and the rest of the Wildlands staff did for him. We know you really helped mold him into who he is today.

All the Best to all of You!

Other Teachers Speak

As mentioned in Chapter 8 "Confidence," we have worked with teachers during the summer to provide a window into our world and how we have managed to develop this learning culture. We always like to hear what the teachers have to say after participating in one of our trainings. We most often get comments like these:

"Wildlands staff and students made the training real, not only in PBL training but also in culture building. Best training I have been to."

"Typically in June my thoughts are as far from school as they can be, but attending the Wildlands Summer Institute left me energized and excited about the coming school year. The staff and students at the Wildlands School described and demonstrated what meaningful learning experiences look like, and I am excited to create those opportunities with co-workers and students at my school."

"Excellent workshop! I greatly enjoyed the opportunities to learn and discuss ideas and experiences. Listening to the students share their projects and being able to work with them on our own projects was a fantastic learning experience. I've come away with a lot of information and ideas that I would like to incorporate into my own teaching."

> "Great seminar. I left feeling excited to make significant change in my classroom."

We truly feel if education is going to move forward and change for the better, it has to start with teachers and schools, and not from some place where policy is debated and lobbyists are the only ones listened to. There is obviously a place for policy change, but real change is when teachers and students do the right things for local communities.

All About People

We believe that much of our educational establishment—the institutions, the policy makers, and the politicians—have forgotten the students are *people*. Those making the decisions and passing the rules and laws are so disconnected with the realities of students that they have no compass to give them real direction. Teachers haven't forgotten the students—they can't—because they are face-to-face every day. For the most part, teachers are some of the most dedicated, caring, and capable people we know. However, teachers are also the some of most over-regulated, controlled, and top-down managed professionals in any workplace. That is where teacher-powered schools can help move schools forward with positive changes for students. In the past thirty years the primary mode and structure of education in our country has changed very little. Other than the technological revolution, many schools are still structured in very similar fashion to those of the early part of the twentieth century. Newsflash! The twenty-first century is already over a decade in and up and running!

We believe that as long as the increasing emphasis is on content standards, high-stakes standardized testing, and homogenization of expectations and delivery systems, the more we distance ourselves from the people who matter most—the students. Learning is an individual enterprise and nobody can do it for anyone but themselves. Having the opportunity to build a school, a learning culture that focuses on the students first as individuals, promotes and teaches teamwork, embeds students in service, and creates an environment where the great majority of the students want to be there every day is not rocket science. If it were, we would have had to use algebra and trigonometry to do it, and we used very little of that. (Just kidding math teachers!) It took listening to the students, creating ways to involve them in relevant, meaningful, and connected pursuits for their learning and throwing out most of the old mold.

Reform that really works means breaking the mold and trying a new one; then reforming, bending, twisting, and retrofitting it as you learn what works and what doesn't. It also is about local control and accountability. Put up or shut up; show us the goods. Be responsible to those who really matter: the students, parents, and communities of our schools. Nobody in some marble building or corporate office with a view can really tell anyone what is good for our schools and our students. Without a way to make decisions firsthand, right there—with the kids—reform is doomed to fail. The old "standards" are just more verbiage, and high-stakes testing for the sake of collecting progress data is flawed.

We know firsthand that every school has strengths and challenges. Schools and teachers can't be everything to everyone, and this means we need more choices to provide for more student diversity and interest. Wildlands is not the answer to global issues in education. It is just a small school, and our story is of how we have been able to work with students as the center of our attention and how we treat them as people. This is the story of how we can change school in ways that tailor it to student needs locally, annually, and even weekly and daily. Our students are not only succeeding in the areas our data-collecting friends value, they are succeeding in the many areas that we are only beginning to design ways to measure.

Essential or Not?

The seven essentials are about transforming school culture, student experience, and creating meaning and context, rather than dictating what students should do or learn in math or English. Obviously, as a school we also value standards that help guide our students to higher levels of competency, skill, and knowledge. Learning standards are important. We use them as guides, measures, and goals. Our students use them when planning projects and within their personal learning plans. There is one big difference, though, when it comes to students and standards. We think it's just as important—or perhaps more important—*how* they get to the target, goal, or standard. We also believe that to learn, grow, and thrive in a school, the school must have an open, safe, and supportive culture that values all individuals involved. We know that **Relationships, Values, Opportunity, Adventure, Challenge, Confidence,** and **Place** can make a huge difference in a school community.

As rare as these seven essential ideas may be in many schools, they are the centerpiece of ours.

TEACHER'S TAKE: LIZ

Reporting Back

One night I ran into a former Wildlands student. This young lady had started at Wildlands as an eighth grader but decided after her sophomore year she wanted to try something different. She wanted more of a traditional social high school experience: a direct connection to extracurriculars, homecoming, prom, and more options for peer and social groups that can be found in a larger student population. She also felt she needed more experience taking notes and preparing for tests, and wanted to make sure she was ready for college.

There were no hard feelings at all when she left. The staff at Wildlands has a simple attitude when it comes to our students: they should do whatever they feel is right for them. We supported her decision wholeheartedly, and I loved checking in with her every time I saw her.

This particular night was in late spring, about one month away from her graduation date. We were having a wonderful conversation, as always, catching up on what was going on at each other's school. She was asking about Wildlands in general, projects that were finishing up, and the plans of each of the graduating seniors. She then told me about her classes, one of her favorite teachers for the year, and her plans for going off to college.

All of a sudden she looked at me and said, "I get it now."

I kind of gave her a scrunched face look, as if to say what do you mean?

"I get what you all were doing each year, especially at the beginning."

At this point I knew she was referring to the staff at Wildlands and the fact that our focus is on the students, not just curriculum.

She continued on, "I used to think you guys were a little crazy having us complete teambuilding activities day after day, or not handing out computers right away or not starting history until there were snowflakes in the air." (She was right. Formal history projects are a winter sport, so we can take advantage of the fall and spring field seasons.)

"After moving from Wildlands to (an unnamed) high school, I can totally see a difference in how the students treat each other and the staff there."

She went on to say something along the lines of the traditional school environment creates an "everyone for themselves" culture. "I see students cheating on tests and homework left and right. They don't care about what they are learning, they only want the A for a grade." She commented that she was really surprised by the "childish" behavior that seemed to go on daily, and the amount of respect that seemed to be missing for each other and the adults in the building. With a bit of a chuckle she said, "There aren't a lot of 'core values attitude' demonstrated by people there."

I continued the conversation by asking her one of my favorite soon-to-be-a-graduate questions, "What do you feel the most prepared for when you think about college?"

She said that she found the things she thought she had been missing at Wildlands like taking notes and tests, and sitting for forty-five minutes at a time, came very easily to her and it wasn't as big of a deal as she thought it would be. She knew she was ready for that. Then, she gave another look and said, "I also understand why you kept telling us over and over that we were in charge. Not of lot of my current classmates have the confidence to believe in their abilities."

There was a twinkle in her eye, and the way that she spoke about her experiences told me this young woman was confident in her abilities and knew she could tackle anything. She credited the Wildlands staff for helping her recognize this. She found she had become a leader in her lab classes like chemistry because she was used to being a problem-solver and solution-finder. She noticed that other students were quick to ask the teacher for help, which meant they were really looking for someone to tell them the answers to the questions, instead of trying to figure things out on their own. She was surprised at how quickly other students would give up. "I now know you were teaching us to believe in ourselves and not have to rely on others all the time."

I think the thing that struck me the most was listening to her talk about her classmates and teachers and how little she knew about each one of them, and they about her. "Very few of the teachers take the time to get to know the students, unless they are popular athletes. It sure isn't a family like it is at Wildlands." She went on to explain that, after spending two years in a building, there were only a handful of people, students and staff, she felt she knew well and how that was drastically different than her time at Wildlands. She also still felt connected to Wildlands and noted that when she would come back from college to visit, Wildlands was the school she was stopping at to check in with.

It didn't really hit me until the next day when I realized how much reflecting she had done about the very different experiences she had in each school environment. When students are faced with big changes in their life, like continuing on with their education at the collegiate level, there are a variety of ways in which educators and adults can prepare them.

The differences between a traditional high school and Wildlands had become very apparent to this young lady. There was competition instead of cooperation, compliance instead of independence, regiments instead of choice and control. Students fought for spots and position instead of working toward common goals, and she realized the only value emphasized was on the end product, the grade, the grade points, and the class ranks, instead of the journey, the students—and the learning.

chapter 11

Forward

So here we are at our "Foreword." We put it at the end because *forward* is the direction we all need to move in education. To move forward, individual schools have to decide it's time to quit doing the same old thing, year after year, decade after decade. Most importantly, we need to ask some new questions, start focusing on local community needs, and for gosh sake, focus on the students!

If we go back to the start of our story and listen to Molly talk about her experience, we hear something all students deserve:

"I came to Wildlands as a junior after spending the previous 16 years at a traditional school. The biggest surprise was being able to say that I love school. Over the course of my two years here, I've developed a passion for learning that I never would have thought possible two years ago."

A passion for learning. That's not found in any of the many reforms and standards handed out over the last few decades. That is where we feel the seven essentials for transforming the way we teach and learn can come in handy. How long has it been since education really looked at itself and changed the game? How can we get people to ask the hard questions and do something different with the students as individuals in mind? When can we focus on developing caring, responsible people with passions for life learning—and growing?

To begin to answer these questions, we need more than reform. We need to *transform* and build anew on successful innovative school models. Every so-called educational reform for decades has been a top-down effort to standardize and streamline learning from the perspective of adults, many of whom have no contact with schools and students. They all have grand proclamations of "How it should be" or "How to be globally competitive," but have they ever actually worked with or even listened to kids? At what point do we realize it's important to actually listen to the kids themselves, especially the many who float through our current system and are not engaged? When do we admit nobody has all the answers, no one system fits all the students, and that education is a journey—not a destination?

Learning is *never* over. It is a daily experience of reflection, growth, failure, recovery, process, and internalization. When the norm is to box it up like cereal on a shelf and ask everything to be testable, we remove the humanity, creativity, imagination, humor, personality, and fun from it. Sure, some parts of education need to be in boxes with high levels of specificity and testing. Obvious things like training to be a doctor or learning to be an electrician or police officer would qualify, but career training is different from general education. If the purpose of general education is to prepare young people to become functioning citizens in a democracy, to build skills and knowledge, to develop attitudes and insight, work ethics and responsibility, and to become interested in learning by discovering their strengths, then we believe the current national education system does not measure up. This is where local change can be effective and successful.

There have been *massive* changes in the areas of new knowledge, technology, and access to information, including web-based delivery and testing systems, and the problem is that *school* hasn't changed much. The one-size-fits-all manufacturing model still prevails. It doesn't really matter whether students are sitting in rows with textbooks or iPads, the mode and culture appear to be the same as it has been for decades. The way children are treated in school has not changed, most of the rules have not changed, the organization of the day, and the compartmentalized courses have not changed. In short, the culture of learning has not changed. To change, you have to DO something differently.

There is often talk about individualization and uniqueness when developing goals for students and schools, but how often do school systems deliver? Every parent, every teacher, and every student should think about what works for each person's success, and insist on a school with a supporting and

4:26 PM MMS

College Biology = Wildlands middle school

4:26 PM

Water quality sampling.

4:27 PM

empowering culture. Too many years in a stagnant system designed over 100 years ago to meet the needs of the people 100 years ago is just too damn many years!

Not changing because it's always been done that way is no reason; it is only an excuse. Letting people who sit on Capitol Hill or in a corporate office decide what is important for our schools and communities is pure craziness. Sweeping "change" from on high is a blanket solution that assumes everyone is the same. When people are completely removed from what happens in real schools, they simply don't understand the realities. *Everyone* has to have a stake in creating new and different schools for our students. When our communities, families, students, and teachers are engaged in meeting the needs of the youth, then strong, vibrant, and successful local schools are built.

In the past ten years, we have discovered that changing the way things are done is really a local issue. Improving the conditions for learning and creating new school cultures is a dynamic, daily process that involves the face-to-face interactions between the most important stakeholders: students and teachers. Having the flexibility to change, the trust to carry it out, and the autonomy to create different types of schools and learning methods is critical for meeting the needs of an ever-changing student population. By no means do we think our experiences are the answer for every school or every student because we understand every school is different and every community has different needs. We just know that the opportunity to change and to do things differently can pay off for the students and teachers because we were fortunate enough to have been given the opportunity to do something different. And it worked.

Ask the hard questions; do something different. Build a place where students value education and relationships they develop with others across generations, and see opportunities instead of assignments. Never be afraid to experience adventures with students, challenge them in ways beyond regurgitating trivial facts, and build their confidence so they know, at their core, that they can be successful. *This* is moving education forward for the kids and their future.

"Doing the same thing over and over and expecting a different outcome is the definition of insanity," is a quote attributed to Einstein or a Texas cattle rancher, depending on your source. Doesn't matter who said it. The message is the same: the challenge to all of us who want better schools, better student outcomes, and real learning is to *make it heard loud and clear that change is okay*. In fact, **essential** change at the core of how schools treat students is required.

Postscript and Invitation

By reading this book, you've gotten an overview of our seven essentials and our ten-year journey to do something really different for students. But the story doesn't end here.

As we wrote this book, we quickly realized the need for Book Two, a "Teacher's Edition" of sorts for *An Improbable School* that includes the nuts and bolts of HOW educators can create—and maintain—a learning culture like Wildlands. The book will include the "down and dirty" details of how everything was actually accomplished at our school, the tricks and systems we've used to implement project-based learning, as well as the myriad of resources we've developed and adapted to make Wildlands a successful student-centered learning culture. We hope you'll continue the journey with us when the book is published. Keep an eye on our website for updates.

Meanwhile, we challenge you to act if you see a need and an opportunity in your community for educational change. A wonderful place to start is the Innovative Schools Network, a group of successful innovative educators across America who are leading the way and have much to offer. For ideas, professional guidance, and support, we urge you to contact the Innovative Schools Network at **www.innovativeschoolsnetwork.com**.

We also encourage you to read *Unsustainable* by Tim R. McDonald and *Improvement and Innovation* by Ted Kolderie, two books that lay out pathways for change and innovation. Indeed, much of what we have been able to do at Wildlands relates directly to ideas these two passionate and forward-thinking educators share with their readers.

Finally, you can find more resources, updates on our progress, and general discussion around our seven essentials at our website, **www.leadthepath.com**. You can also contact us there directly to arrange speaking engagements, coaching, seminars, training, or consulting.

We look forward to hearing from you!

The Catalyst

Project Foundry™

Project-Based Learning Made Easy

www.projectfoundry.org

How does one empower students and manage the uncommon learning along the path? **Project Foundry** is a web-based management platform for students and teachers. The tool was built specifically to enable the kind of learning environment that serves the needs of the next generation rather than the one of the past.

Contact **Project Foundry** to schedule a demo and receive a free trial. Mention *An Improbable School* to redeem a special offer.

info@pblhq.com
877.836.9960

INNOVATIVE SCHOOLS NETWORK

Transforming education one school at a time.

A nonprofit, 501(c)(3) organization led by professional educators, the Innovative Schools Network (ISN) supports the establishment and growth of high quality, research-based innovative schools by providing professional training and guidance, and ensuring that educators can easily collaborate, connect, and learn from one another.

The ISN supports school innovation in these three pillars:

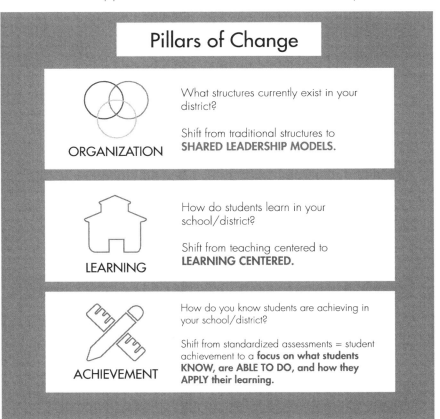

Pillars of Change

ORGANIZATION

What structures currently exist in your district?

Shift from traditional structures to **SHARED LEADERSHIP MODELS.**

LEARNING

How do students learn in your school/district?

Shift from teaching centered to **LEARNING CENTERED.**

ACHIEVEMENT

How do you know students are achieving in your school/district?

Shift from standardized assessments = student achievement to a **focus on what students KNOW, are ABLE TO DO, and how they APPLY their learning.**

nnovativeSchoolsNetwork.com

Acknowledgments

As an author team, we need to thank many individuals and groups for their efforts and support in the development of the school—and in our path to publishing this book.

First and foremost, we thank the incredibly talented team of individuals we have had the privilege of building Wildlands and working with over the past ten years: Co-founder and middle-school guru, Jeff Hadorn; our wilderness guide and comic relief, Jake Fields; and our indispensable school grandpa, Chuck Forseth, all of whom have been crucial members of the Wildlands School team. We also want to recognize the Augusta School District administration and school board, the administrative support and clerical staff, transportation staff, and food service staff for their help over the years. The partnership with our sponsoring district has been unwavering, rewarding, and provided the autonomy and trust necessary to become a teacher-powered school and to create a new model for student-learning communities.

We also feel it necessary to mention the teachers everywhere who have influenced our lives, including all the friends and colleagues we've met and worked with along the way. There are far too many to list, but you know who you are. We have worked with and learned from hundreds of amazing teachers over the years, and we are very grateful for the mentoring, interaction, and collaboration. A special thank you to the schools and organizations we first visited for ideas, clarification, inspiration, and reassurance before our doors were open. They paved the way for innovation and we cannot thank them enough for their guiding light.

From the beginning, the members of the original planning committee and those who have served on the Wildlands governance board have been our strongest supporters. Without these people, the vision would not have become a reality. We would also like to thank the Fall Creek School District administration and school board and the Beaver Creek Reserve board of directors and staff for partnering with our school district in the development, support, and sustainability of Wildlands simply because they knew it was the right thing to do for kids.

It would be remiss not to recognize and thank the innovators and trailblazers in education who see the need for a change in education, and take the risks necessary to provide students with relevant, meaningful experiences. None more so than Shane Krukowski and the Project Foundry team for their vision in developing a management system for organizing project learning and remaining committed to keeping students at the forefront of their own educational experience.

We cannot forget to thank organizations and agencies that have allowed our students to gain real-world experience by working side by side on community projects, including everyone who has donated time, resources, and funding to support Wildlands School. Special thanks to the Wisconsin Department of Public Instruction (DPI) Charter School office and staff for guidance and support throughout our formative years.

When it comes to writing this book, there are some very gifted people who have supported us and lent their expertise on this journey. We have to start with the extremely dedicated staff of the Innovative Schools Network (ISN), especially Heather Terrill Stotts, ISN executive director. Heather has been our biggest supporter, cheerleader, confidant, and gave countless hours to this project. Without her assistance, we would not have reached our goal.

Our gratitude and appreciation goes to two multi-talented individuals who have helped us bring these words to life. Thank you to Michelle Watkins for helping us streamline our story, and to Chris David for all the creativity in the design, and additional editing, too.

An enormous thank you also goes to our families, mostly our spouses, Dawn Tweed and Brian Seubert, and children, for dealing with the long hours, time away, and understanding our need to follow a passion we wholeheartedly believe in for over ten years. Your support has been tremendously appreciated and never overlooked.

And finally, the biggest thank you goes out to ALL of the Wildlands students and families for their belief and trust in our vision, mission, and abilities. Nothing would have been possible without you. We are deeply grateful—and proud—to be on this journey of shared learning with all of you.

What teachers are saying about
An Improbable School:

In my 15 year entire teaching career I have never come across a school that has such ⟨ positive culture of respect and student ownership. This book is a reminder of the real reason we all became teachers.
Jeremy "Pete" Peterson, Teacher, Northern Lakes Regional Academy

"An Improbable School" has truly set the Gold Standard for other project based schools in a myriad of ways: the incredible staff, driven students, culture of curiosity, summer institutes project sharing, and open-door policy to name just a few. Whether you're looking to start ⟨ school, as we were, or improve an existing finely tuned program, reading this book is a must
Matt Weege, Teacher, 7 Rivers Community High School

"An Improbable School" is committed to the idea that culture building and the processes o⟨ inquiry and design are not secondary to "academic" content. Tweed and Seubert describe ar environment for students that we long to provide (and work in) as teachers, managers anc parents. Their environment fosters the creation of self motivated individuals that don't nee⟨ to be managed, can work in teams and problem solve confidently.
Todd Brunclik, Founder/Advisor, Birchwood Blue Hills School

Paul and Liz were instrumental in the development and start-up of our charter school. Theii expertise in creating a school where students have a voice and value their own education is second to none.
Joel Dziedzic, Principal & Director of Next Generation Learning, Wayne Elementary School

---

For information contact:
Paul@LeadthePath.com or Liz@LeadthePath.com

Editor: Michelle N. Watkins
Cover Design: Roslin Media
Interior Design: Chris Lorette David

20287865R00084

Made in the USA
San Bernardino, CA
05 April 2015